Devotions for the
Blended
Family

"But as for you, continue in what you have learned and have become convinced of . . ." (2 Timothy 3:14)

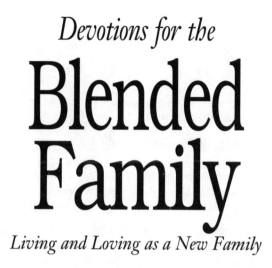

Devotions for the

Blended Family

Living and Loving as a New Family

Margaret Smith-Broersma

Grand Rapids, MI 49501

Devotions for the Blended Family
by Margaret Smith-Broersma.

Copyright © 1994 by Margaret Smith-Broersma.

Published by Kregel Resources, an imprint of Kregel Publications, P.O. Box 2607, Grand Rapids, MI 49501. Kregel Resources provides timely and relevant resources for Christian life and service. Your comments and suggestions are valued.

Cover Photograph: © THE STOCK MARKET/
                  Jon Feingersh 1994
Cover Design: Tammy Johnson/FLAT RIVER GRAPHICS
Book Design: Alan G. Hartman

Library of Congress Cataloging-in-Publication Data
Smith-Broersma, Margaret, 1952
    Devotions for the blended family: living and loving as a new family / Margaret Smith-Broersma.
       p.   cm.
    Includes bibliographical references and index.
    1. Family—Prayer-books and devotions. 2. Remarriage—Religious aspects—Christianity. 3. Stepfamilies.
I. Title.
BV4526.2.S535   1994   249—dc20   94-17861
                                            CIP

ISBN 0-8254-2150-0 (paperback)

1 2 3 4 5 Printing / Year 98 97 96 95 94

Printed in the United States of America

About This Book

Not all families are blended in the same way or for the same reason, but if you are that kind of family, this family devotional guide will be a helpful resource to further your new family's growth.

All Scripture references are from the *New International Version* unless otherwise indicated.

Some of the ideas in Devotions 27 and 28 came from *Leading Little Ones to God* by Marian M. Schoolland.

A Note to Parents

This book is for you to read with your children to help your entire family grow with one another and with God. Please use discretion about which entries may or may not be suitable for your particular family at a specific time—on the other hand, please don't be afraid to use this book as a tool for the discussion of difficult subjects.

To Olivia, who didn't keep my idea a secret,
and to my family—without them there
couldn't be this book.

Devotion 1

Scripture:

To appoint unto them that mourn . . . to give unto them beauty for ashes, the oil of joy for mourning, the garment of praise for the spirit of heaviness; that they might be called trees of righteousness, the planting of the Lord, that he might be glorified (Isaiah 61:3 KJV).

We are so thankful for our new beginning. Out of our loneliness and pain God brought comfort and healing, but only now that we are together does it seem that we are totally alive again, totally whole. He took our heavy, empty hearts and filled them with new love and new loves! He has blessed us with a new family—a blended family—and we are full of joy and are excited for what lies ahead.

Five-year-old Lisa's words summed up how we all felt when on a day shortly after our engagement, she hopped into the car and declared, "I can't wait to marry you guys!" And that's what we did. We all married each other.

Let's Talk:

What is this going to be like? What do you think?

To Learn More:

To read additional verses for a new marriage, see Mark 10:6–9 and 1 Timothy 5:14.

Prayer:

"Dear Father, You have been so good to heal our wounds and to bless us by bringing us together. It's exciting, but scary, too, as we face a new life and make a new family together. Thank You for being with us every day and for giving us the love with which we can love one another. In Your name, amen."

Devotion 2

Scripture:

. . . to bestow on them a crown of beauty instead of ashes, the oil of gladness instead of mourning, and a garment of praise instead of a spirit of despair. They will be called oaks of righteousness, a planting of the Lord for the display of his splendor (Isaiah 61:3).

As our friends and family have watched us and seen our mourning turn to gladness and our despair to praise, God says that He will make us like mighty oaks and He will do this to display His power! What a challenge for our family—our specially-blended family—to be referred to as a family so strong in faith that we are like mighty oak trees! He wants to display His healing power through us.

Sometimes, as the days go by in our new life together, we may not feel much like "mighty oaks," but we know that God is at work in us. The same power that turns a small acorn into a strong oak tree can turn our small faith in Him into strong faith. Then, when other people see what God can do in us, they will praise Him!

Let's Talk:

What does it mean to display His power? How can our family do that? How does our faith display God's splendor?

To Learn More:

For more about God's healing power, read Isaiah 30:26 and 2 Thessalonians 3:3.

Prayer:

"Dear Lord, help us to faithfully glorify You. Lots of people are looking at us to see how we're going to do this job of blending our families. When they see us, help them to see Your power in us and see that You are the one making this family "work." Truly make each one of us like mighty oaks of faith that You may be glorified. Amen."

Devotion 3

Scripture:

But now, this is what the Lord says—"Fear not, for I have redeemed you; I have summoned you by name; you are mine" (Isaiah 43:1).

In all our excitement and anticipation to make a new family, in all our eagerness to "make it better," there is something that we can never ever forget. No matter how blended we become, how well it goes for us, how many new and wonderful memories we create, how happy we are, and even if after a long time other people don't know that we are blended—we ARE a blended family and that's what we'll always be. There will always be another mom who gave birth to some of you and another dad who fathered some of you. They are forever a part of our lives—that's just the way it is in our family. God has still called us; we are His children. And He put us together and He made us what we are—a blended family.

Let's Talk:

What are some of your happiest memories of your other mom or dad? Share them with the family.

To Learn More:

For more about the wonder of God's plan, read 1 Corinthians 2:8–10.

Prayer:

"Dear heavenly Father, help us to respect one another's memories of our past families. May we always be able to share in stories and remember together, and may we have understanding that as much as we love each other, there are two moms and two dads in these kids' hearts, and that's okay. Thank You. Amen."

Devotion 4

Scripture:

So do not fear, for I am with you; do not be dismayed, for I am your God. I will strengthen you and help you; I will uphold you with my righteous right hand (Isaiah 41:10).

When we married, we didn't just blend our families—we blended all our rules and expectations—wow! We have certain expectations and preconceived notions that, without even thinking about them, have carried over from having been families with a different mom or a different dad. The first time the new dad or the new mom doesn't behave in the old, predictable way—the way the other one did—it kind of throws us for a loop. It kind of scares us. We feel insecure because we don't know why he or she is acting like that. We have been so glad to find each other, and we still are. But it's scary too. "Why are you angry? My other dad liked it when I acted that way. We thought we were having fun together." "My other mom didn't expect that of me, why do you?"

Let's Talk:

What are some things that you feel scared about in our new family? What are some things that make you feel mixed up? Let's talk about them and see if we can make them less scary.

To Learn More:

Here are some more verses about not being afraid: Psalm 91:10–11 and Psalm 91:4–7. Read them if you have time.

Prayer:

"Dear Lord, please help us learn to live together. Please be our teacher. Please help us treat each other with patience and understanding and compassion. Amen."

Devotion 5

Scripture:

If any of you lacks wisdom, he [or she] should ask God, who gives generously to all without finding fault (James 1:5).

Two boys and a mom, three girls and a dad. How can this group learn to live in the same house with one another after twelve years and fifteen years of living with someone else? How can we start to feel like one family? Who gets the privilege of being the oldest now that there are two "oldests"? And do a boy and a girl the same age but in different grades have the same privileges? This was "their" house, now it is "our" house. How do we make it "ours" without "them" feeling like they are losing something? God does promise to give wisdom to know how to live. But how can He give wisdom to us in all of this?

Let's Talk:

Is there one thing that you wonder about now that we are together? Lets talk about it.

Let's remember to ask Him to help us understand each other and to know how to make this new family work.

To Learn More:

Some more verses about wisdom can be found in John 14:16–17 and Psalm 25:12.

Prayer:

"Dear Father in heaven, You know and we know that we need Your wisdom to bring this all together. Thank You for the great promise that You've made to give wisdom to all who ask. We are asking. Thanks for answering. Amen."

Devotion 6

Scripture:

These commandments that I give you today are to be upon your hearts. Impress them on your children. Talk about them when you sit at home and when you walk along the road, when you lie down and when you get up (Deuteronomy 6:6–7).

In this family we love God, and we want to treat each other the way He would like to see us treat each other and live the way He wants us to live. But in order to do that, we have to know what the Word says about things. So, when we have a problem getting along or when we have to make a decision about what is right or wrong for this family and the children in this family, we will try to remember to first think about what God's Word tells us.

If we have a fight or an argument (which we will because we aren't perfect), we need to solve it in a way the Bible shows us. If we have a problem at school with another kid or a teacher, we can pray together about it and think about what God's Word says would be a good way to deal with it.

Let's Talk:

Do you feel embarrassed to ask God for wisdom with your problems? Do we need to feel that way? How can we use the Bible as our guide book in our relationships, at home and at school and at work?

To Learn More:

To read more about the wisdom to be found in the Bible, read Proverbs 4:10–14.

Prayer:

"Dear God, please help us to always live for You. Help us to remember to talk things over with You, to ask You for wisdom, and to look in Your Word for guidance. Thank You for Your Word. Amen."

Devotion 7

Scripture:

Do not merely listen to the word, and so deceive yourselves. Do what it says. Anyone who listens to the word but does not do what it says is like a man who looks at his face in a mirror and, after looking at himself, goes away and immediately forgets what he looks like (James 1:22–24).

When we look into God's Word and see instructions on how to live, and we notice that we are not doing what it says and we don't change our behavior, we are like a person with a dirty face who looks in the mirror and then goes away without washing it and even forgets that it's dirty. That isn't a very wise thing to do, is it?

God's Word is full of information on how to live. There is the moral law (called the Ten Commandments). There are proverbs, with all kinds of advice on how to relate to others and how to follow the right path. The stories of Jesus and the letters of the apostles give us a lot of ideas about personal holiness and how to relate to people, especially in the church. But none of this is of any use whatever unless we do what it says.

Let's Talk:

Can you remember one time when you had to consciously decide whether to obey God or not? Share it with us if you would like.

To Learn More:

To read more about the importance of obeying the wise instruction of the Bible, read Proverbs 4:20–27.

Prayer:

"Dear Lord, please help us understand how to live for You. Teach us to obey Your Word. Holy Spirit, please give us the power to obey. Amen."

Devotion 8

Scripture:

If we confess our sins, He is faithful and just and will forgive us our sins, and purify us from all unrighteousness (1 John 1:9).

For if you forgive [others] when they sin against you, your heavenly Father will also forgive you (Matthew 6:14).

We have lived together long enough to know that we aren't perfect, none of us. And not only do we get impatient with each other and argue with each other, but sometimes we do disobey God's Word. Someone may tell a lie. Have you? (Answer to yourself only.) Someone may be mean and selfish when God says love one another. Have you? (Answer to yourself only.) Someone may have broken any one of the commandments. But 1 John 1:9 is SO GREAT! It promises us that no matter what, when we confess our sins—that means when we agree with God that we have done wrong—and we are sorry, we can ask God to forgive us and He will! Then we need to remember to ask each other's forgiveness too.

Let's Talk:

Has anyone ever asked you to forgive something he or she said or did? What did you say?

To Learn More:

For more verses about forgiveness, read Hebrews 4:14–16.

Prayer:

"Dear Father, please forgive us our sins, and may we quickly, without holding grudges, forgive those who sin against us. In Jesus' name, amen."

Devotion 9

Scripture:

Carry each other's burdens, and in this way you will fulfill the law of Christ (Galatians 6:2).

It's so wonderful to have a big family, and to have so many to share our burdens and to pray for us. When one of you comes home after a terrible day at school, we can *all* empathize, and pray together, and maybe even offer some ideas for problem solving. It was great the other day when we all prayed for Dad's problem at work, and then he came home and told us how well it was solved. When things are getting too much for Mom, we can all pitch in and do extra to help out. If homework is too tough, Dad or Mom can give advice
When someone picks on one of you at school
ne defends you, you are bearing one another's
it great to have a big family for sharing and
ust to tell our problems to, but to pray with us
y feel with us?

some ways a big family can share and support

More:

y like to read Romans 12:9–15 to gain even more encouragement for helping each other.

Prayer:

"Lord, thank You for our wonderful big family. Please help us to be there for each other, to always accept and support each other, that You may be glorified. Amen."

Devotion 10

Scripture:
Love each other as I have loved you (John 15:12).

The other day, Lisa slipped into the creek. While not threatened with drowning, she was wet and cold; the banks were slippery and she couldn't get out. Others around her were afraid of getting wet and cold, too, and hesitated about helping her. Without so much as a thought for himself, her new brother Aaron reached in and pulled her out, and everyone cheered. Aaron was loving Lisa more than he was worried about himself.

Let's Talk:
Is there an example here for us? What does it mean to love each other the way Christ has loved us? What are some other ways that we can show this kind of love?

To Learn More:
To read more about how to treat one another with love, you may want to read Romans 12:16–21.

Prayer:
"Dear Lord Jesus, please help us to love each other the way You have loved us, with self-sacrificing love. Strengthen the bonds of family loyalty and family caring, and make us a family who truly loves one another the way You have loved us. Holy Spirit, fill us so that it will be You loving through us. For Jesus' sake and for God's glory we pray. Amen."

Devotion 11

Scripture:

For waging war you need guidance, and for victory many advisors (Proverbs 24:6).

". . . and in multitude of counselors there is safety" (Proverbs 24:6 KJV).

Sometimes it feels like war around here. We want our *family* to be the winner, we want "us" to win, not one person. But some days we just don't understand the battle. On those days, Mom just does not understand Tammy. When she thinks she has Tammy's reactions and likes and dislikes figured out, there is nothing but rejection and maybe a big blow-up. Mom feels like she can never please Tammy. And Tammy may try, but feels like she can't please Mom. Sometimes Dad just can't do anything right for Aaron, and Aaron can never do anything right for Dad. We have talked and talked and prayed and prayed. We think it's time for more advice. It's time to get some help from a counselor. There is a counselor that specializes in blended families and we are so glad that we have the opportunity to get help.

Let's Talk:

In what ways do you think a counselor might help us?

To Learn More:

Even Moses needed wise men to help him lead Israel. You can read about his story in Exodus 18:13–27.

Prayer:

"Dear Father, thank You that there is help and support for our kind of family. Thank You that we are not in this alone. Not only are You with us, but You have provided trained professionals who can give us more wisdom. Help us to be honest. Help us to learn. Help us to blend with love. Thank You. May we give You the glory. Amen."

Devotion 12

Scripture:

Call unto me, and I will answer thee, and show thee great and mighty things, which thou knowest not (Jeremiah 33:3 KJV).

It only took a few weeks, a few visits with the social workers, and Mom and Dad began to understand a lot more. Tammy and Aaron began to understand some things too, and with all the understanding, the communication got a lot better. We made some giant leaps in our relationships and in our blending as a family during that spring and summer. Throughout the second school year of our marriage, Tammy and Aaron met with the school social worker off and on. He helped them work on their relationship and decide how to both be the oldest together. By the end of that year, they were pretty good friends and have been ever since. We asked God for help, and He led us to others with more insight than we had. All of us learned "great and mighty things" that improved and strengthened our entire family.

Let's Talk:

Do you need this kind of wisdom in your family? Ask everyone to think about it. If you are afraid to ask for help, remember, it can be a great way to come to understand "things you do not know," as the *New International Version* translates this verse.

To Learn More:

In Isaiah 42:16, God promises to give His children wisdom for walking "unfamiliar paths." You may want to read this verse for further encouragement.

Prayer:

"Dear Jesus, help us not to be afraid to ask for help when we need its. Lead us to the right person for help. Open our hearts and minds to learning things that we don't understand. Make us what You want us to be. Amen."

Devotion 13

Scripture:

The fruit of the Spirit is love, joy, peace, patience, kindness, goodness, faithfulness, gentleness and self-control (Galatians 5:22).

When going from having only two or three children to suddenly having five, Mom and Dad just did not know automatically and instantly how to deal with the changes. Sometimes Mom thought Dad was being mean to her kids, and sometimes Dad thought Mom was expecting way too much from his kids. And besides the pain of seeing our kids hurting, there was the pain of feeling division in our family. So, we worked out a code. If either of us thought the other was coming down too hard, we would ask, "May I see you in the bedroom?" There we would immediately say what danger we thought we saw. Usually it's best to let the natural parent do the disciplining, but realistically, he or she just isn't always there or doesn't always notice the problem. A lot of talking and explaining has to happen. We have to talk a lot to the children and to each other so that we will understand each other's motives and heart.

As time has gone on, this part has become less and less an issue. We have gotten used to each other. And over the long haul, we have seen just as much love and attention handed out as discipline and punishment. Because we have more of a history with each other now, our trust has grown. And we understand that both parents have the kids' best interests at heart.

Let's Talk:

Kids, can you tell that this is how we feel? Do you believe you are loved?

To Learn More:

The Spirit provides the self-control we need in being stepparents. For additional strength, read 2 Peter 2:2–8.

Prayer:

Lord, we need Your help, always. Thank You for helping us. Amen.

Devotion 14

Scripture:

Children, obey your parents in the Lord, for this is right. "Honor your father and mother"—which is the first commandment with a promise—"that it may go well with you and that you may enjoy long life on the earth" (Ephesians 6:1).

In the beginning of our blended family, a day came when each parent had to say, "I know you had a different mom/dad before you had me. But I am the mom/dad of this house. Because I am the mom or the dad of THIS house, you must obey what I say. You may love your other mom or dad. I expect that you will. But here and now WE are the bosses, WE are the authority that God has placed here. We will try to listen to what you have to say and discuss it if we can. But obeying us is the only way it will work out for us as a family here."

Let's Talk:

Did you know that God promises to bless you for obeying your parents? What is the blessing in the verse above? Did you know that our policies and rules are made because of what we think is best for you?

To Learn More:

The writer of Ephesians was referring to the fifth commandment. If you have time, read that commandment in Exodus 20:12.

Prayer:

"Dear Father in heaven, please help our children to obey and to feel the security and love that results from knowing the limits and obeying them. Please help us as parents to be fair and loving. Thank You for being the perfect example of parenthood. In Jesus' name, amen."

Devotion 15

Scripture:

He who scorns instruction will pay for it, but he who respects a command is rewarded (Proverbs 13:13).

We parents have set family policies and rules that we think are the best for our family. Things like chores, individual responsibilities, curfews, acceptable and non-acceptable ways of relating to each other are all designed for your individual welfare and for the good of our family.

Let's Talk:

What do you think the verse means by "to scorn instruction"? In what ways will a person pay for it? (Hint: A lot of our hard times, especially as young people, are caused by some of the choices we make and the things we do.) What do you think the verse means when it says "respecting a command will be rewarded"? (Hint: In our house, the more responsibly you behave and the more obedient you are, the more we trust you with extra privileges and freedoms.)

To Learn More:

Proverbs 4 gives us a lot more reasons to listen to our parents. It is full of promises for the obedient and warnings for the disobedient. Read as much of it as you have time to read.

Prayer:

"Dear Father in heaven, please help our children to listen and obey so that they may be rewarded, both now and in their future lives. Help us parents to obey Your Word too, especially in the standards we set and the way we raise our family. In all that we do, in how we live, may we bring glory to Your name. In Jesus' name, amen."

Devotion 16

Scripture:

The sacrifices of God are a broken spirit; a broken and contrite heart, O God, you will not despise (Psalm 51:17).

Sometimes when we do something wrong, we think we have to make up for it. We think we have to do a whole bunch of good stuff in order for God to forgive the wrong. But God says that rather than sacrifices, He looks for a broken and contrite heart. If our heart is really broken over our sins, if it is truly repentant (repentant is what *contrite* means), then He will forgive us. Okay, so what does *repentant* mean?

Being repentant doesn't just mean to be sorry for the wrong things we've done, although being sorry is a part of it. Maybe a good way to understand what the Bible means by "repenting" is to think of getting lost while driving in the car. We have to recognize that we are going down the wrong road and that we need to change directions so we can get to where we need to be. Repentance means to change your mind and the direction of your life from that of self-centeredness or sin-centeredness to God or Christ-centeredness. If my heart is broken over my sin, so broken that I turn my behavior—my whole life—around, toward God, then I have repented and God forgives me.

Let's Talk:

Have you ever been "broken and contrite" over your sins or over a certain specific sin? Do you feel that God has forgiven you?

To Learn More:

For more about repentance, read Acts 3:19 and James 4:8–10.

Prayer:

"Dear Jesus, thank You for dying on the cross for my sins. Please help me to obey You. In Your name, amen."

. . . .

Scripture:

For if you forgive men when they sin against you, your heavenly Father will also forgive you. But if you do not forgive men their sins, your Father will not forgive your sins. (Matthew 6:14–15).

Sometimes when another person, especially a brother or a sister, has violated our rights—you know: taken something without asking, broken something of ours, betrayed a confidence (that means telling something personal and private to others), embarrassed us in front of others, really awful stuff like that—it's VERY hard to forgive! But God says that we MUST forgive them. If we don't, why should He forgive us?

If we are grateful that God has forgiven us for the wrong things that we have done, if we are grateful that He doesn't hold a grudge against us for violating His rules for living, and if we believe that he has totally and completely forgiven us because Jesus died for our sins, then we must forgive others.

Let's Talk:

Let's talk about something that was really hard for you to forgive. Is there something that you still need to forgive a brother or a sister for doing to you? Isn't this as good a time as any to say "I'm sorry" and "I forgive you?"

To Learn More:

You can read more about forgiving others in Matthew 18:21–22.

Prayer:

"Dear Father in heaven, please help us to love one another and to forgive, even if it means forgiving over and over. Help us to love one another enough that we won't keep violating each other's rights. In Jesus name, amen."

. . . .

Devotion 18

Scripture:

My command is this: Love each other as I have loved you (John 15:12).

While we were still sinners, Christ died for us (Romans 5:8).

Wow! When did Christ love us? While we were still sinners. That means that even before we thought about being sorry for our sins, He was already loving us and had already come to die for us. We need to love each other even when the other may not be exactly lovable. Have you ever noticed that when you are the grouchiest is when you need the most love? When things are tough at school or if you feel pressured or when Mom and Dad feel pressure from work or deadlines, that's when we need to know that our family members stand by us and care for us and love us. But man, what a job! It's not easy to love a grouch. And not every one of us needs the same kind of love when we are low. One of the things you can do to make me feel better when I'm feeling tense and pressured is to be extra-helpful or to surprise me with a hug. But not every one of us would like that.

Let's Talk:

Can you tell about a time when you tried to love one of us even when that person was grouchy? Did it work? Let's talk about what each person needs from the rest of the family when he or she is in a bad mood.

To Learn More:

1 Corinthians 13 is called "the love chapter." You may like to read it to learn what true love is like.

Prayer:

"Dear Jesus, help us to love one another in the same way that You love us—even when we don't deserve it. Thanks. Amen."

Devotion 19

Scripture:

"No one who puts his hand to the plow and looks back is fit for service in the kingdom of God" (Luke 9:62).

I can do everything through him who gives me strength (Philippians 4:13).

Sometimes we may feel that we want to go back to the lives we had before. It was easier to have fewer kids in one house, and it was easier to live with the same set of parents and siblings that we were born with. This blending two families into one can be hard sometimes.

In our family, we didn't feel that being a single-parent family was very great, so we would not want to go back to that. But sometimes we do think of the days when we were the original family with the original mom and dad and wish it could be that simple again. Even though it may have seemed easier, it just isn't one of the choices we have. The other mom and dad are not coming back. We need to look ahead and to know that it will get easier and easier. We can do *all things* through Christ who gives us strength—even blend! God promises to help us and He will.

Let's Talk:

Can you think of some of the things we have already gotten used to about each other? Lets talk about some of them. See how much progress we have already made? And we will get more and more used to each other.

To Learn More:

In Isaiah 41:13 God promises to give us help and strength. If you have time, read this verse for more encouragement.

Prayer:

"Dear Jesus, thank You for helping us get more and more used to each other. Thank You for giving us strength to do all things. Amen."

Devotion 20

Scripture:

"If you love me, you will obey what I command" (John 14:15).

"If anyone loves me, he will obey my teaching . . . . [A person] who does not love me will not obey my teaching" (John 14:23–24).

A few days ago, we talked about being sorry for our sins and what repentance is. We said *repentance* is making a change. After being sorry for the wrong things I have done, if I decide to quit doing them and follow God's way, I have repented. (Sometimes we still mess up, but that's another story.) How important is the repentance part? Isn't it enough to just be real, real sorry? Jesus said that if we love Him, we will obey what He says. And if we don't obey God's Word, we don't love Him. This is very heavy stuff. Although we are not perfect, do we try with all our hearts to obey what we know God wants for us?

Let's Talk:

Can you share something that you are sorry for and that you have tried not to do again? We can pray for each other and ask God to help all of us to obey Him with all of our strength.

To Learn More:

Read James 2:14–26 to learn more about how doing right proves our faith.

Prayer:

"Dear Lord Jesus, please help us to love You more all the time, and to show that love by our obedience to You. Holy Spirit, please send Your power to give us victory over sin in our lives. For Your glory we pray. Amen."

Devotion 21

Scripture:

The Lord is faithful to all his promises and loving toward all he has made (Psalm 145:13).

Have you ever noticed that when we really love something, it's easy to take care of it? When children have pets they love, they show their love by feeding, watering, petting and generally caring for those pets. If moms and dads love their children, they will care for them. Children may lose interest in their pets after awhile and forget to take care of them. Some moms and dads are not good parents and don't take good care of their children. But God never loses interest in us or fails to care for us.

This verse reminds us that God made us, and because we are his creation, He is loving and faithful to us, always keeping all His promises. Can you name some of the promises of God? Let's see if we can each share one or two of the ways that God has kept His promises to us.

Let's Talk and To Learn More:

If you can't think of any of God's promises off the top of your head, here are Scriptures that contain a few of them. Look up as many of the verses below as you have time for, and in each one see what God promises His children in that verse.

John 14:18	Deuteronomy 31:6	1 John 4:18
Psalm 46:1	Isaiah 41:10	Psalm 23:4–5
John 14:1	Romans 8:35–37	Romans 8:15
Romans 8:38–39	Matthew 28:20	Hebrews 13:6
1 Peter 5:7	John 16:22	Psalm 91:4–7
Psalm 9:9–10	John 14:27	Isaiah 43:2
Psalm 91:10–11	2 Timothy 1:7	Psalm 27:1

Prayer:

"Dear Lord, thank You for Your faithfulness. Thank You that You love us and that You keep Your promises. Amen."

Devotion 22

Scripture:

Submit to one another out of reverence for Christ. Wives, submit to your husbands as to the Lord. Husbands, love your wives, just as Christ loved the church and gave Himself up for her (Ephesians 5:21–22, 25).

Did you kids ever wonder why Mom and Dad have a date every week? Sometimes do you feel jealous because we don't take you along? If you do, or if you feel like you want to interfere when we are sitting alone and talking quietly, just remember: without our marriage, there is no blended family. A family begins when a man and a woman become united to one another in love and with the commitment of marriage. When we married before, it was just two people, and we had some time to work on our relationships before the kids came. But now, we married and all of you were already here! So, we need those times alone. We need to love each other and spend time making our love grow in order for our family to be strong. A speaker I heard on the radio said, "The greatest thing a man can do for his children is to love his wife." When you see our love for each other, we hope that it will make you feel safer and more secure, because you know that our family is as strong as our marriage.

Let's Talk:

What are some topics you think Mom and Dad need to talk about when they're alone?

To Learn More:

You may want to read Genesis 2:18, 24 and Matthew 19:4–6. They explain further about how men and women need one another and that marriage is of God.

Prayer:

"Dear Father, thank You for marriage and the family. Thank You for bringing us together and helping us learn how to love one another. Amen."

Devotion 23

Scripture:

Your attitude should be the same as that of Christ Jesus. (Philippians 2:5).

Whatever is true, whatever is noble, whatever is right, whatever is pure, whatever is lovely, whatever is admirable—if anything is excellent or praiseworthy—think about such things (Philippians 4:8).

Sometimes we let you watch certain TV shows and not others, and tell you to turn the TV off when you'd rather not. This verse is why. Our minds are like computers. Whatever we put in is what we get out. What we want to see coming out of your lives is a lifestyle and way of speaking that is pleasing to God, that is obedient to His Word. It is not possible to obey God without filling our minds with Christ. It is not possible to please God if our minds are filled with wrong ways of thinking.

Let's Talk:

Let's talk about some of the TV shows that we don't like for our family to watch. Can you see how the messages of those shows is not noble, pure, right, and lovely? What are some of the messages in the world around us, that we see every day, that are not excellent, noble, right, pure, and lovely? Besides not thinking on certain things, what are the noble, true, pure, lovely, excellent things that we can think on?

To Learn More:

Psalm 139:23–24 is a prayer that David prayed for God to search his heart and thoughts. You may want to look it up and use it instead of the prayer below.

Prayer:

"Dear God, help the mind of Christ my Savior live in me each and every day. Amen."

Devotion 24

Scripture:
Read Psalm 102:1–11.

When a parent leaves because he or she dies or because of a divorce, it hurts a lot. You have each had that kind of pain, and maybe you still feel it sometimes. When you are missing your other mom or dad, you may feel like crying or getting really mad. It's okay to cry, and it's okay to feel angry. You can try to get rid of your anger by walking, running, playing, or working hard. Another thing that may help you feel better is to find someone you love and then talk about how you feel with him or her. Maybe that person is sad or angry, too. Maybe you can cry together. We hope that you can talk to us. But if you can't, we will try to help you find someone to talk to. God understands how you feel, and He loves you even when you are angry or sad. Often we feel His understanding and love through other people.

Let's Talk:
Can you think of a time when God showed His love to you by loving you through another person?

To Learn More:
You may want to read Psalm 102:12–13. It tells how God hears our cries for help, has compassion, and will show His children favor in His time.

Prayer:
"Dear Lord, please heal our hurts, and help us to be comforted by Your love and our memories. It is hard to lose someone we love. Thank You that You will never leave us or forsake us. In Jesus' name, amen."

Devotion 25

Scripture:

He who dwells in the shelter of the Most High will rest in the shadow of the Almighty. I will say of the Lord, "He is my refuge and my fortress, my God, in whom I trust" (Psalm 91:1–2).

God is our refuge. He is always there for us in our times of hurting and our times of happiness. But do you notice the first part of the verse? It says "he who dwells." That means we must decide where to live our lives. Do we dwell with God? Have I asked Jesus to forgive all my sins and have I placed my life in God's hands? To whom do you give your life? (Answer silently to yourself.) Do you give it to God? Or, do you want to keep your life for yourself? If you have given your life to Him, then it can be said that you are dwelling in "the shadow of the Almighty." He becomes your refuge, the One to whom you can run with any problem or trouble. To have the Lord for your refuge and fortress, to have a heavenly Father in whom to trust, is the safest, securest, most wonderful place to rest your heart.

Let's Talk:

Can you think of a time when you ran to your heavenly Father when you had a problem or trouble?

To Learn More:

Read Romans 8:35–39 for more reassurance.

Prayer:

"Dear heavenly Father, we pray that all of the children in this family will dwell in You, and find You to be the shelter, the refuge, and the fortress that You promise to be. Thank You. Amen."

Devotion 26

Scripture:

For what I want to do I do not do, but what I hate I do. . . . What a wretched man I am! Who will rescue me from this body of death? Thanks be to God—through Jesus Christ our Lord! (Romans 7:15, 24–25).

The apostle Paul sometimes had a hard time doing what he knew was right. Sometimes it is so much easier to do the wrong thing than the right thing. He says in Romans 7 that this is because he has a basically sinful nature. But even though there is this struggle inside between doing what is good and right and doing what is bad and wrong, Paul praises God that through the power of Jesus Christ he can do the right thing. When we are faced with this struggle, we must remember, like Paul, that the power to do right comes from Jesus Christ our Lord. We can ask Him, and He will give us the strength to do right.

Let's Talk:

Have you ever had a tough time doing the right thing, and then, after asking God to help and strengthen you, you found it easier? Share these times with each other.

To Learn More:

2 Corinthians 12:9–10 gives more reassurance that God is our strength. Read it if you get a chance.

Prayer:

"Dear Holy Spirit, please fill us. Enable us to obey Your Word, and to please You in all that we do. Thank You. Amen."

Devotion 27

Scripture:
"You shall have no other gods before me" (Exodus 20:3).

We have talked a lot in this book about believing in God, asking Jesus to forgive our sins, and living for God. But not everyone believes in the God of the Bible. Deep down in every heart, there is an empty place, a need. Some people who feel this need in their hearts answer God and say, "Yes, I want to be your child." Other people feel the empty place inside and try to make their own gods. Some people pray to the stars, sun, or moon. Some people build idols out of wood or stone. But these kinds of gods can't hear or answer us when we pray. Some people make sports or getting more money or succeeding at a certain job or having just the right kind of house or clothes the most important thing in their lives. Whatever is the most important thing in your life is your god. But none of these things fit into that empty space the way God does. We need God. He is the only One who can fill the empty place because He made us, and that empty place is just for Him. He wants to be the most important thing in our lives.

Let's Talk:
Can you describe the empty place in your heart? How do we know there is an empty place down in our hearts until we ask God to fill it with Himself?

To Learn More:
Read Matthew 6:33 for further meditation.

Prayer:
"Dear God, please help each one of us to keep You, every day, as the most important thing in our lives. Please help each person in this family to invite You into our lives to fill the empty spot and help us to live for You. Amen."

Devotion 28

Scripture:

"God is spirit, and his worshipers must worship in spirit and in truth" (John 4:24).

"You cannot see my face, for no one may see me and live" (Exodus 33:20).

Sometimes we may think it would be so much easier to believe if we could just see God. But nobody has ever seen God. We cannot see God because He is spirit. God made us with a body and a spirit (also called a soul). Your spirit is the "real" you. Nobody can see your spirit, but it's there, inside. God is all spirit, without a body. That's why we can't see Him. But He sees and hears and loves us. God is so awesome that if we could see Him, it would kill us! He is so perfect and so holy and so powerful and so full of glory that a human being just couldn't take the shock of seeing God. In Exodus 33, there is the story of Moses, a man who got very close to God. The Bible says that after being very near to God for a few days, Moses' face shone with such a bright light that the people who saw him could not even look at his face without being blinded by the glare. And that was without looking on God's face!

Let's Talk:

Do you sense that there is a "real you" down inside your body—a "spiritual" you?

To Learn More:

To hear the story about Moses, read Exodus 33.

Prayer:

"Dear Heavenly Father, please help us to have faith. Help us to believe. In Jesus' name, amen."

Devotion 29

Scripture:

For since the creation of the world God's invisible qualities—his eternal power and divine nature—have been clearly seen being understood from what has been made, so that men are without excuse (Romans 1:20).

Believing in God, who we can't see, is called faith. If we can't see God, how do we know He exists? For the next few days, we will talk about some of those ways.

One of the ways we know God exists is through His creation. Psalm 19:1 (KJV) says, "The heavens declare the glory of God; and the firmament [earth] showeth his handiwork."

When the boys and I lived in Florida, we loved to go to the beach. Sitting on the sand under a brilliant blue sky and watching the endless tide and limitless horizon never failed to fill me with peace. It seemed no matter how deep my discontent or anxiety, the infinite character of God would fill me with comfort and hope.

When our family traveled out West and saw the gorgeous Black Hills, and majestic Mount Rainier and when we hiked in the mysterious Badlands and camped in the awesome Glacier National Forest—in all these places we saw God's creative hand and the power of His divine nature being revealed. In all of those places at night, as well as our own back yard, we can look up and see the evidence of God's existence and gain a sense of His vastness from the star-studded sky. We can hear God saying to us, "I am!"

Let's Talk:

Let's remember and share some times our family, before or after we got together, saw God or felt God in his handiwork. Then use your imaginations. Based on what you have seen in creation, how would you describe God?

To Learn More:

To hear more about the presence of God in creation, read Psalm 19:1–4 and Job chapters 38 and 39.

Prayer:

"Dear Lord, make us sensitive to Your hand in creation. Help us to see all that You have made, know that it is good, and worship and praise you for it. Amen."

Devotion 30

Scripture:

Open my eyes that I may see wonderful things in your law (Psalm 119:18).

The man without the Spirit does not accept the things that come from the Spirit of God, for they are foolishness to him, and he cannot understand them (1 Corinthians 2:14).

Besides showing Himself in creation, God has made Himself known by speaking directly to a few people throughout time. Adam and Eve in the book of Genesis, Samuel in the books of Samuel and Kings, and the prophets Elijah and Elisha are some of the people to whom God spoke directly. We can learn about God and what He expects of us and what He wants us to do by reading their stories in the Bible.

All of the Bible is God's Word to us. When we read the Bible, God is talking to us. When we go to church and listen to our pastor read and explain the Bible to us, God is talking to us. When we read the Bible during family devotions, God is speaking to us. We read our Bibles often because we want to know what God is saying to us. But none of what the Bible says will make any sense to us unless we have the Holy Spirit in us, helping us to understand what it says. We can ask God to fill us with His spirit, so that we can read the Bible with understanding.

Let's Talk:

Have you ever had trouble understanding something in the Bible? Have you ever asked God's Spirit to help you understand? Did it make a difference?

To Learn More:

The book of Jude, verses 17–19, tells more about how the natural person cannot understand God and how we should act to those who doubt.

Prayer:

"Please give us understanding hearts, Lord, to understand Your Word to us. Amen"

Devotion 31

Scripture:
Come before him with joyful songs. (Psalm 100:2).

God is our refuge and strength, a very present help in trouble (Psalm 46:1 KJV).

Sometimes we know God is real simply because we can feel His presence. We often feel His presence in church when we lift our hearts in singing. We feel His presence when others pray for us. In our family, we can remember the grief and sorrow when our loved ones died and how many, many people prayed for us. At that time we could feel the Lord to be very near. In our first days of grieving, the presence of God was so real we almost felt that we could touch Him. Some of the other times that we may feel God's presence are when we pray and when we quietly read His word.

So we sometimes know that God is real because we feel Him with us. There are times when we may not feel Him at all. His Word assure us that in those times, He is there also, keeping His promises whether we feel Him or not. (see devotion number 21 for assurance of His presence). But feeling God near is one way we know that He exists.

Let's Talk
Have you ever felt the presence of God? Share it with us. If you have not ever felt His presence, talk to Him in prayer, and tell Him that you want to know His presence in your life.

To Learn More
Read Psalm 46:1–7 for further meditation.

Prayer:
"Lord fill us with Your Spirit. Help us to know that You are real by a sense of Your presence with us. In Jesus name, amen."

Devotion 32

Scripture:
Know that the Lord is God (Psalm 100:3).

For the last few days we talked about how we know that God is real. We said that we know that God is real because we can see Him through the wonders of creation. We also know that God is real through the record of people to whom He spoke in the Bible. And yesterday we said we can know that God is real because sometimes we feel His presence. Now we will take a few days getting to know the character of God according to what the Bible says about Him. We talked before about the fact that God is a spirit. Do remember what a spirit is? (You may go back four pages if you need some clues.) But God is more than a spirit. He has many qualities, all of which are important to know if we want to know God.

We can get to know a lot about His character by listening to the many different names for Him in the Bible. Each one of the verses below gives one of God's names. Let's read as many of them as we can.

Let's Talk and To Learn More:
Can you see how we can know God through His many names?

Genesis 2:4	Deuteronomy 33:27	Jeremiah 32:18
Genesis 14:18–22	Joshua 3:10	John 1:9
Genesis 28:3	Psalm 80:7	Matthew 6:26
Exodus 3:14	Isaiah 43:3, 14	1 Timothy 1:17
Genesis 15:2, 8	James 1:7	1 Timothy 6:15

Prayer:
"Lord, give us spiritual eyes that we may know You in a very real way. Help us to hear and understand Your character as the Bible teaches it. Help us to feel Your presence. In Jesus' name, amen."

Devotion 33

Scripture:

Lord, you have been our dwelling place throughout all generations. Before the mountains were born or you brought forth the earth and the world, from everlasting to everlasting you are God (Psalm 90:1).

Through good times and bad times, God is there, and we may dwell in Him. Before the world was, there was God, and forever without end, there is God. WOW! God has no beginning and no end. Something with no beginning and no end is called *infinite*. God is infinite. It makes you and me feel pretty small when we think about the vastness of God's being. On the other hand, how it makes us marvel to think that He, this infinite God, has opened His arms to us and said that we may dwell in Him. If we have chosen the God of the Bible as our God and placed our lives in His hands, then God is our dwelling place. There is a great deal of security in knowing that the infinite God is our refuge at all times, both good and bad. We can go to Him to talk. When we come before Him by reading His Word, praying, or worshiping, it is as if we are held in His arms. I love having the infinite God for my dwelling place.

Let's Talk:

Do you think you understand what it means to "dwell in God"? Lets talk about it. Do you have a feeling, a sense of belonging to Him?

To Learn More:

For further meditation, read Ephesians 3:14–20.

Prayer:

"Dear Father God, may we dwell in You, and may Your Spirit dwell in us. In Jesus' name, amen."

Devotion 34

Scripture:

Where can I go from your Spirit? Where can I flee from your presence? If I go up to the heavens, you are there; if I make my bed in the depths, you are there (Psalm 139:7–8).

For a [person's] ways are in full view of the Lord, and he examines all his paths (Proverbs 5:21).

God is everywhere. No matter where we go on earth, under the earth, above the earth, God's Spirit is with us. When we are hurting or afraid, when we are over-flowing with joy, in all things and at all times, God is there. If we need comfort and strength, we are so glad to know that Jesus is with us. As little children we learned the verse: "When I am afraid, I will trust in you" (Psalm 56:3). But when we are not doing as we should, when we want to do the wrong thing, when we desire to sin more than we desire the approval of God, He is with us then too! He sees us!

Let's Talk:

How does knowing that the Lord sees me in all places and all times change what I may do or think about doing? How does knowing that Jesus is always there help me when others are pressuring me to do something I know I shouldn't?

To Learn More:

Read all of Psalm 139.

Prayer:

"Lord, help me to live like someone who is always in the presence of the Lord. Help me to receive Your comfort when I am afraid or hurting, help me to ask for Your help and strength when I am tempted to do wrong. In Jesus' name, amen."

Devotion 35

Scripture:

Holy, holy, holy is the Lord God Almighty, who was, and is, and is to come (Revelation 4:8).

God was reconciling the world to himself in Christ, not counting men's sin against them (2 Corinthians 5:19).

God is holy. That means that He is utterly and entirely perfect. He never has and never will do anything wrong. Remember when we talked about Moses, who saw God from behind, and afterwards, his face shown so brightly that no one could look at him? That was the purity and holiness of God reflected on Moses. Remember when we talked about how we often do wrong even when we know better? Because we do wrong, (sin) and God never does wrong, we are separated from God by our wrong. God cannot look upon our sin any more than the people could look on God's holiness. But God has a solution for this problem of our being separated from Him. The solution is a sacrifice sent to take the punishment for our sin, for everything that we have ever done wrong. Jesus Christ died on the cross to take the punishment for us so that we would no longer be separated from God. If we believe that Jesus died on the cross to pay for our sins, and if we have gone to Him and asked forgiveness, then we are *reconciled* with God. That means we can now have a relationship with Him. We can communicate with God and He with us. We can now "look" at each other, because our sin is taken away and God's holiness is now part of us.

Let's Talk:

In what ways do we communicate with God after He has forgiven our sins?

To Learn More:

For further meditation, read John 3:15–18.

Prayer:

"Lord Jesus, thank You for dying for me. In Your name, amen."

Devotion 36

Scripture:

For God is greater than our hearts, and he knows everything (1 John 3:20).

. . . Christ, in whom are hidden all the treasures of wisdom and knowledge (Colossians 2:2–3).

God knows everything. God knows what we are like because He created us. He knows what we do and how we feel. He knows how it may hurt that one of our parents went away, and He knows how tough it can be to live in a blended family with a stepparent and maybe stepbrothers and stepsisters. But He doesn't just know, He loves us (1 John 4:19) and He cares (2 Corinthians 1:4), and as we have said before, He is always there. If it seems that no one else can understand how we feel, God can.

Let's Talk:

Are there times lately when you haven't felt that anyone can understand you? Let's talk about those times.

If we end up frustrated because we don't understand each other we can at least pray together. God, who understands and knows us so well, promises to help us be wise concerning one another (James 1:5–6). This may be one of those kinds of times when your family (like ours) may need to talk to an expert outside the family.

To Learn More:

For further meditation on the wisdom of Christ, read 1 Corinthians 4:5–11. For more about God's all-knowing nature, read Isaiah 40:12–17.

Prayer:

"Dearest Father God, please help all of us to understand each other. Please help us to care and love the way You do. Thank You for hearing us and for answering our prayers. In Jesus' name, amen."

Devotion 37

Scripture:
God hath spoken once; twice have I heard this; that power belongeth unto God (Psalm 62:11 KJV).

God is all powerful. We said before that God is the Creator. Because He is the creator of all things, He has power over all things. He is the designer of the universe, the originator of the laws of nature. At any time God may intervene in the natural order of the things He has created, He may disturb the laws of nature and cause miracles. One of the miracles that we read about in the Old Testament is the day the Lord made it stay daylight way longer than it should have. The Old Testament prophet said it was the day God "made the sun stand still." (You can read the story in Joshua 10.) Only God could do this sort of miracle. In Exodus we read about the miracle of the Israelites crossing the Red Sea (Exodus 14), the plagues on Egypt (Exodus 7–12), and miracles done by the prophets, especially Elijah and Elisha.

Let's Talk:
What are your favorite miracles from the Bible?

To Learn More:
Read one of the events in the Bible mentioned above.

Prayer:
"Dear Heavenly Father, thank You that You are more powerful than Pharaoh in Moses' time, and thank You that You are more powerful than the most evil people today. Thank You that You have a plan, and that even though bad things happen, You are in control. Help us to trust in You. In Jesus' name, amen."

Devotion 38

Scripture:

And Jesus came and spake unto them, saying, "All power is given unto me in heaven and in earth" (Matthew 28:1).

When we think about the word "power," we might think of a person with really strong muscles like Arnold Schwarzenegger or an olympic weight-lifting competitor hoisting thousands of pounds. We may think of a big truck plowing through mud or winning a tug-of-war with another truck in the power competitions shown on TV. But even the person with powerful muscles can't control everything, and motors and machines can't do anything without people to make and operate them. No one or no thing in this world is all-powerful. But Jesus says in this verse that He has ALL power.

Believing that God is all-powerful leads us to some hard questions. If God knows everything and is everywhere and has all power, then why does He let bad things happen? Why did my mom or dad die? Why didn't my parents stay married? Over the next several days, we will talk about why bad things happen.

Let's Talk:

Why do you think bad things happen?

To Learn More:

For further meditation on the power of God, you may like to read Romans 11:34 and Job 40 and 41.

Prayer:

"Dear Jesus, please help us to understand, as much as we can, why bad things happen. Give us faith to trust You when we don't understand and make us wise enough to take the pain and suffering and make it be something good in our lives. For Your glory we pray this, amen."

Devotion 39

Scripture:

We also rejoice in our sufferings, because we know that suffering produces perseverance; perseverance character . . . (Romans 5:3).

Being confident of this, that he who began a good work in you will carry it on to completion until the day of Christ Jesus (Philippians 1:6).

One result when bad things happen is the development of our character, making us each the kind of person God wants us to be. If we have problems that cause us to have to wait for something we want, perhaps we will learn patience. If we have limited financial resources, we can learn to be more creative with what we do have and learn good bargain-hunting skills. If school is hard for us, we can give up, or we can develop self-discipline and perseverance of a kind that people who have life easy will never know. When people are struggling or hurting, sometimes that is when they find God. Some of you would not have met Jesus if your parents had not divorced or died. Some of you have learned to turn to God more because of the pain and hurts of life.

Let's Talk:

Can you think of one or two ways that your life or your character (the real you) is better because of the bad thing that happened? Do you think this could be a part of God's plan for you? If you can't think of how any good can possibly come of what has happened to you, wait on the Lord in prayer, ask Him to show you.

To Learn More:

For further meditation, read Romans 5:1–6.

Prayer:

"Lord Jesus, help us to take our trials and use them to make us better people. Amen."

Devotion 40

Scripture:

We also rejoice in our sufferings, because we know that suffering produces perseverance; perseverance, character; and character, hope. And hope does not disappoint us, because God has poured out his love into our hearts by the Holy Spirit, whom he has given us (Romans 5:3–5).

When I was a young mother with two little boys, ages four and six, I had to have open-heart surgery. When I first found out I needed this operation, I was angry with God for not healing me. I knew there was a chance that I might die. My greatest worry was if I were to die, who would raise my children? In the weeks preceding my surgery, I learned a valuable lesson, a lesson that never left me: "Trust those children to God. If you die, it is part of His plan for the kind of people He is making them to be." Well, I didn't die. But I did learn to trust my children to God. I learned to trust that He knew what was best for my boys, even better than I knew. And God knew how much I would need that trust when, two years later, their father died. If I had continued to be angry and bitter about my surgery and had not learned to trust God with my children at that time, how much harder it would have been to trust them to Him at the time of their father's death! God was preparing me for the unknown future with a lesson that I hardly wanted to learn, but a lesson that became my greatest comfort at a time of even greater pain.

Let's Talk:

Can you think of anything that you learned from something bad that happened to you? Could you use this lesson later? Have you ever seen the way you can learn and grow from bad things that happen?

To Learn More:

For more comfort in bad times, you may want to read Psalm 91:4–7.

Prayer

"Dear Lord, help us to learn from the bad things. Help us not to waste our pain but to allow something beautiful to grow from our suffering. For Your glory we pray. Amen."

Devotion 41

Scripture:

"If anyone chooses to do God's will, he will find out whether my teaching comes from God . . ." (John 7:17).

We have said that sometimes bad things happen that result in our character development. Bad things sometimes happen because God created each of us with the ability to make choices, a free will, and we don't all choose right all the time. Remember how in an earlier lesson we learned that sometimes the good in us "wars" against the bad in us? God allows us to make choices, and many of the decisions we make get us into trouble. If we didn't have a free will, we would love and serve Him like robots who were programmed by their designer.

In the very beginning of creation, in Genesis 2, God gave Adam and Eve a choice about whether to obey Him or not. He gave them only one rule, they chose to disobey it, and sin entered the world. It was the choice they made. Later, they were sorry, and God began the preparations to pay for sin by foretelling the sending of a Savior (Genesis 3:15). God wants people to serve Him and obey Him because they love Him and because they choose to obey. Sometimes bad things happen because people use their free wills to do evil rather than good.

Let's Talk:

Can you see the importance of being created with a free will? Can you think of a time when something bad happened to you because of your own choices or actions?

To Learn More:

You may read about the first effects of free will to make choices in Genesis 3 and 4 and God's solution in 1 Corinthians 15:21–22.

Prayer:

"Dear Father in heaven, help us to understand Your ways. And when we can't understand, help us to trust in You. Amen."

Devotion 42

Scripture:

"You intended to harm me, but God intended it for good to accomplish what is now being done, the saving of many lives" *(Genesis 50:20).*

"For I know the plans I have for you," declares the LORD, "plans to prosper you and not to harm you, plans to give you hope and a future" (Jeremiah 29:11).

The first verse above was spoken by Joseph to his brothers. They had sold him into slavery, and he had had some pretty awful years. But then Joseph's position in Egypt was used to save all of God's chosen people during a time of famine. God took something evil and used it for good. The second verse assures us that God has good plans for His children, plans that bring hope and give us a future. If you have trouble finding any good or purpose in the trial you are going through, cling to the promises of God. If you have a hard time thinking with hope about the future, one of the things you can do is fill your mind with Scripture. You many want to use the references listed in Devotion 21 to do this.

Let's Talk:

Let's talk about some of the things that may be hard for you to accept in your life. As we share them, let's pray about them and pray for each other to believe God has a good purpose. We are not powerless when we can pray!

To Learn More:

For further meditation, use the Scriptures found in Devotion 21.

Prayer:

"Dear Jesus, we are not our own, we belong to You. Please help us to believe You have a good plan, even when we can't see. In Your name, amen."

Devotion 43

Scripture:

Trust in the Lord with all your heart; and lean not on your own understanding. In all your ways acknowledge him, and he shall direct your paths (Proverbs 3:5–6 KJV).

This is one of the greatest promises of God. You see, whether God is directing our paths (guiding our lives) doesn't depend on how we feel or how badly things are going. God has promised to never leave us. We must not depend on whether we see God or understand what He's doing. We must trust in His promises. Sometimes, in the worst of times when we don't even sense God's presence, we must use our minds (not our feelings) and remind ourselves that He is directing our paths.

Trust God's Word and God's promises, not your own feelings.

Let's Talk:

Have you ever felt that God had left you? Share that time with the family. Can you look back and see that He was at work in your life? Maybe you are in that kind of tough time right now. We can pray for each other and remind one another of the promises of God.

To Learn More:

For further meditation, read Psalm 27:1; 31:19–20, and Psalm 32:7.

Prayer:

"Dear Father God, please help us to believe that the plans You have for us are best and that You are directing our paths, even when things are not going well and we are tempted to stop trusting. Thank You that Your promises are true, no matter how we feel. In Jesus' name, amen."

Devotion 44

Scripture:

For our struggle is not against flesh and blood, but against the rulers, against the authorities, against the powers of this dark world and against the spiritual forces of evil in the heavenly realms (Ephesians 6:12).

Another reason bad things happen is because there really is a battle going on all the time between good and evil. There is evil all around in the world in which we live. The verse above talks about the struggle we have against the spiritual forces of evil. Because there is disease in the world, some people get cancer. Because there is alcohol in the world, some people get drunk and then use their own free wills to drive while drunk and then they may hurt others. There are men and women with evil ideas who put those ideas into books, movies, and even TV shows. Others read or watch and then use their free wills to do the evil that they have learned. For our part in the continuous battle of good and evil, we can "resist the devil" and "put on the full armor of God."

Let's Talk:

Can you think of evil that you have seen or heard around you lately? Have you ever been tempted to do a bad thing that you saw on T.V. or in a movie? What do you think is meant by "the full armor of God"? We will talk more about the armor of God in a few days.

To Learn More:

For reassurance that Christ is stronger than evil, read Hebrews 2:6–9.

Prayer:

"Dear Jesus, protect us from evil. Teach us how to put our lives into Your hands so that whatever happens, we know that Your plan is being done. Help us to use our free will to make choices for good and not for evil. Thank You for Your power and Your might. For Your glory we pray. Amen."

Devotion 45

Scripture:
. . . the Father of compassion and the God of all comfort, who comforts us in all our troubles, so that we can comfort those in any trouble with the comfort we ourselves have received from God (2 Corinthians 1:3–4).

When my husband (Aaron and Andrew's father) died, we were filled with grief. It was a pain and a sorrow like nothing we ever felt before. Many of our friends prayed for us, sent cards to us, and many people came to us to comfort us with their hugs and their words. It all was a comfort. Their prayers helped us feel God's comfort, God's presence. But the most comfort we received was from those who had also suffered grief and loss. It seems that there is no comforter like one who has "shared in our suffering." They know how we feel. Comfort from those who have also hurt is a special sort of comfort. I don't think that God makes us suffer just so we can comfort others, but we can use the experience of our own suffering to bring hope and healing to others.

Let's Talk:
Can you think of a time you comforted someone because you had experienced the same thing?

To Learn More:
For further reflection, read 2 Corinthians 1:1–11.

Prayer:
"Lord, help us to open our hearts and our arms to others who are hurting, help us to turn our pain into something positive. In Your name and for Your glory we pray. Amen."

Devotion 46

. . . .

Scripture:

Dear friends, do not be surprised at the painful trial you are suffering, as though something strange were happening to you. But rejoice that you participate in the sufferings of Christ, so that you may be overjoyed when his glory is revealed. If you are insulted because of the name of Christ, you are blessed . . . (1 Peter 4:12–14).

Sometimes we experience difficulties because we are Christians. Have you?

The apostle Peter wrote these verses in a letter to his friends, Christians who were scattered all over Europe. Some of them had to leave their homes because they had become followers of Jesus Christ. Sometimes they felt discouraged and sad to have left their homes and to have others mock them. Have you ever been mocked because you believed something different than the people around you? Maybe you believe that you must not harm your body with drugs or alcohol, and others mock you for it. If you are a Christian who is serious about obeying God's law and you plan to save sex for marriage, you may get ridiculed for that. Sometimes it is not easy to be a Christian and have Christian standards when it seems like everyone else is doing those things.

Peter wrote this letter to encourage those early Christians who got mocked, and his words can encourage us too. He tried to show them how to have victory over suffering. One thing he reminded them of is that Jesus their Savior had suffered much much more. If Jesus who they followed suffered, they should expect that it would happen to them, too.

God is concerned with our souls, our spirits, and with whether or not we are becoming like Him. Verse 13 says that if we suffer for Christ, we will be "overjoyed when his glory is revealed." We may suffer right now, but some day we will share in God's glory; we will have eternal life. Like the old hymn says, "it will be worth it all, when we see Jesus."

. . . .

Let's Talk:

Can you think of a time when someone made fun of you because you are a Christian?

To Learn More:

To learn more about what Peter said to the suffering church, read all of 1 Peter 4.

Prayer:

"Lord, help us to not be discouraged if we are mocked, but help us remember that as You suffered, so will we. Help us to be faithful in that suffering and to look ahead to the day when we will be completely free of suffering in the glory of Your presence. Amen."

Devotion 47

Scripture:

I consider that our present sufferings are not worth comparing with the glory that will be revealed in us (Romans 8:18).

Wait for the Lord; be strong and take heart and wait for the Lord. (Psalm 27:14).

Some day, all our suffering will seem worthwhile when we see Jesus. Today's verses are just more reminders of what we talked about yesterday—promises from God that all suffering is temporary and that God will strengthen us for whatever trial we are experiencing. The time will come when all wrongs will be righted and wronged ones will be vindicated. It is really tough to hang on to promises like this that may seem so far in the future. But the happiness and peace of someday being with Jesus will be greater than any of the suffering we go through now.

Let's Talk:

What are some of God's promises for the future that are well worth waiting for?

To Learn More:

For further mediation, read Romans 8:18–28.

Prayer:

"Dear Lord, it is hard to hang on sometimes when we suffer. Please show us how You are at work in our suffering, making us more like You, and help us to feel the sureness of the promise that one day we will be with You. Thank You for the comfort that Your Word gives to us now. In Jesus' name, amen."

Devotion 48

Scripture:

My flesh and my heart fail, but God is the strength of my heart . . . (Psalm 73:26).

I can do everything through him who gives me strength (Philippians 4:13).

Often, in the middle of going through a huge pain or a terrible problem, we feel that we simply cannot bear any more. But that is when God becomes our strength. We are right when we say, "I just can't take it anymore." We can't. But that is when, as we gradually let Him have His way in us and with us, He becomes our strength. Problems and sufferings that we know we cannot endure can be born when we allow God to be our strength.

When I was a widow and Aaron and Andrew didn't have a dad, sometimes I thought I couldn't stand being alone another minute. But I did stand it. God was with us. When Roger was a widowed father and all the girls got sick at the same time, he thought he couldn't stand it. But he cried out to God and he still remembered in his darkest days how without a wife, he really wasn't alone. God sent him the help that he needed. If the trials are more than we can bear, perhaps it is because God is trying to tell us that we must learn to do things not in our own strength, but "through Christ." Christ is the One from whom we can get our strength.

Let's Talk:

When have you felt most alone?

To Learn More:

You may read Psalm 38:9–15 to learn of David's hope in the Lord at a time when he felt his strength was gone.

Prayer:

"Dear Lord, please help us to come to You for strength. Teach us that the only way to be faithful and obedient in the world in which we live is to do everything in Your strength. Thank You for giving us that strength. In Jesus' name, amen."

Devotion 49

· ·

Scripture:

"My flesh and my heart may fail, but God is the strength of my heart and my portion forever" (Psalm 73:26).

In our house we have two cedar chests. Although we don't like the fact that they use up space, we have determined to keep them because in those chests are mementos, possessions of our children's deceased parents. The girls have enjoyed wearing their birth mother's earrings at times and using the same blanket for ball games that she used. Aaron shaves every day with his birth father's razor and shaving cup, saved for him in a chest until he needed it. There are other things in those chests: pictures, jewelry, medals, and other "portions" of a life our children once lived with that parent. As special as these things are to us, they are not as important as the portion that is spoken of in Psalm 73.

King David says in this verse that God is his "portion forever." He is talking about his inheritance. In David's time, the land a person inherited was just about the most important thing in his life. The land would determine his lifestyle and wealth. God Himself, David says, is the most important thing for which David longs.

Do we long for God as if He alone were our "portion"? Is God the most important thing? Sometimes we have trials so that we can learn to long for God more than anything else. When we long for God, He comes to us and brings us the strength we need to go on when we think we can't.

Let's Talk:

Have you ever longed in your heart for God? Have you ever just wanted to feel His presence more than anything? God promises, "Call to me and I will answer you" (Jeremiah 33:3).

To Learn More:

For further meditation, read Psalm 73:23–28.

Prayer:

"Dear Lord God, help us to call out to You. Help us to learn to always make You our strength and the most important person in our lives. Thank You that You are there for us even when we feel alone. In Jesus' name we pray, amen."

· ·

Devotion 50

Scripture:

"I have told you these things, so that in me you may have peace. In this world you will have trouble. But take heart! I have overcome the world" (John 16:33).

How comforting and secure it is to know that despite the fact that we will inevitably have trials, tribulations, problems, and pains, Jesus, the One in whom we put our hope, has overcome all of those things. What do you think it means to "overcome"? When Andrew plays videos games, he talks about "mastering" certain levels and certain games. In order to master a game, he has to be able to conquer, or win, against many different challenges to his skill. As his skill in a certain game increases, he will conquer a challenge, and then finally, with much time and effort he will finally master the game. It's the same way with bad habits or evil in our lives. The more we work at it, the better we will get at overcoming.

Do you have a sin that gets you every time? Are there bad words that you just can't seem to quit saying? Are there sinful thoughts that you just can't seem to quit thinking? Is there a disrespectful attitude in your heart against one or both of your parents that you just can't seem to get rid of? Jesus says that "in me you will have peace." If we live on our own in the world, we will not be overcomers and will not have peace. But if we place our lives "in Jesus," we can have peace inside ourselves because He is at work, helping us "overcome the world."

Let's Talk:

What do you think it means to "overcome"? Have you ever overcome?

To Learn More:

For more about the strengthening presence of the Holy Spirit which brings us peace, read John 14:23–26.

Prayer:

"Dear Lord, please rule over our lives. Help us each day to place ourselves in Your hands. We ask for the peace that only You can bring as You overcome the world in us. Thank You. Amen."

Devotion 51

Scripture:

Finally, be strong in the Lord and in his mighty power. Put on the full armor of God so that you can take your stand against the devil's schemes. . . . Therefore put on the full armor of God, so that when the day of evil comes, you may be able to stand your ground . . . (Ephesians 6:10–11, 13).

There are times in our lives, times we could call "the day of evil" when we are tempted to do what we know is wrong. Sometimes the temptations are so strong that we may feel like there is evil all around us. We talked before about Isaiah. These verses tell us that if we put on "the full armor of God," He will make us strong, so that we can stand up against the evil forces around us. Another kind of "evil day" was when death came to our loved ones, by disease in one case and the drunkenness of a driver in the other. Our other mom and other dad had given their lives to God, and they went to heaven where they live now in perfect joy. But we were hurt by the disease and the sin, the evil, that touched our family. We learned at that time that we could be strong in the Lord. He was there to help us.

Let's Talk:

Has there ever been a time in your life when you felt evil all around you? Did you feel like you wanted to do wrong? How did you fight it? Or have you experienced the other kind of evil, when you felt like bad things were happening to destroy you, to break your heart? God offers us His armor when we must be strong in battle. We will talk about the first piece of that armor tomorrow.

To Learn More:

Read Psalm 27:14 and 2 Samuel 10:12 for two more verses about how God makes us strong.

Prayer:

"Lord, make us strong, with Your mighty power. Help us to always stand against evil. In Jesus' name, amen."

Devotion 52

Scripture:

Stand firm then, with the belt of truth buckled around your waist (Ephesians 6:14).

[Jesus said] "Sanctify them by the truth; your word is truth" (John 17:17).

The first part of the armor of God mentioned in Ephesians is the "belt of truth." For the people of Palestine in Bible times, a belt was more than just the decoration that it often is for us. When a man prepared for action, he lifted his robes, tucked them into his belt, and tightened the belt. In this way he was ready to move about quickly, to move unhindered. Our truth is the Word of God. If we know the truth about what God says in His Word, the truth about right and wrong, the truth about God's promises, then we can be strong when we are tempted to do wrong, and we can rely on the promises of God with confidence because we are sure of what we believe. If our minds are filled with the truth from God's Word, we will be ready to take action against the devil. If our minds are filled with truth, the thoughts and ideas from the world and Satan that tempt us to do wrong simply will not have room to remain in our thinking.

Let's Talk:

What are some examples of God's truth that can be filling our minds?

To Learn More:

For more understanding of the belt of truth, read Exodus 12:11 and Luke 12:35. To learn more about the way truth can win over sin, read John 8:31–38.

Prayer:

"Dear Father, makes us strong in Your truth. Help us to listen and learn when we hear Your Word taught. Help us to understand the truth of Your Word through the power of the Spirit, and to 'be strong in the Lord and power of His might.' Thank You. Amen."

Devotion 53

Scripture:
. . . with the breastplate of righteousness in place (Ephesians 6:14).

Dear children, do not let anyone lead you astray. He who does what is right is righteous . . . he who does what is sinful is of the devil (1 John 3:7–8).

The second piece of the armor of God mentioned is the breastplate of righteousness. A suit of armor has a breastplate strapped across the chest, protecting the heart. In Ephesians 6, the belt of truth and the breastplate of righteousness are mentioned in the same verse. This is because if our minds are filled with truth, we will begin to act like the truth that we know; we will become righteous. We will be strong against the devil and against temptations. It's as if our hearts are protected from evil by the righteousness that comes from knowing the truth. When temptations to do wrong come like arrows aimed at our hearts, our hearts are protected with the breastplate of righteousness that we have put around us because we know the truth as it is found in God's Word.

When someone tries to get us to do wrong, it will be easier to resist if our minds and hearts are filled with God's truth.

Let's Talk:
Do you notice a difference in how easy or how hard it is to do what is right depending on how often you listen to God's Word? If you take time to read God's Word, and pray, are you stronger against evil? Is it easier for you to do good if you are listening to the truth in God's Word? Does it become tougher to do what is right if you haven't spent time listening to God?

To Learn More:
To think more about being righteous, read 1 John 3:10.

Prayer:
"Lord, help us to surround ourselves with Your truth, to remember that Your Word is truth, and truth is what brings us righteousness. In Jesus' name, amen."

Devotion 54

Scripture:

. . . and with your feet fitted with the readiness that comes from the gospel of peace (Ephesians 6:15).

When a Roman soldier prepared for battle, he put on firm-soled, high-laced foot gear with nails or spikes in the bottom. He wanted to make sure that he would have a solid foothold no matter what the surface of the battleground was like. And he wanted firm support so his foot would not move around inside of his shoe, causing wobbling and twisting. He wanted to stand firm and be prepared for the battle by what he put on his feet. Modern athletes wear special footgear, too, designed to help win the "battle." Football players wear well-fitted shoes with spikes on the bottom so if the ground is wet, they can dig in and take a firm stand when the "enemy" tries to tackle them. Baseball players and golfers also have cleats on the bottoms of their shoes so like the Roman soldiers of Bible times, they can get a firm hold where they stand.

If we are firmly grounded, if our feet are "planted" firmly in the truth that comes from God's Word, we will be able to be strong and not wobble or slip when we are tempted to do something wrong.

Let's Talk:

What are some of God's firm truths to tie onto our feet?

To Learn More:

For more about the feet of those who believe the gospel, read Romans 10:14–15.

Prayer:

"Dear Lord, help us to faithfully stand in the truth of Your Word. Keep us "rooted and grounded in the Word of the Lord" so that we will always be ready to take a firm stand against evil when we are confronted with it. In the power of Your Son's name we pray, amen."

Devotion 55

Scripture:

In addition to all this, take up the shield of faith, with which you can extinguish all the flaming arrows of the evil one (Ephesians 6:16).

Did you ever see the movie *Ben Hur*? There is a scene from that movie that shows Roman soldiers on the front lines of battle advancing by picking up a huge shield, as big as a door, and crouching behind it. When they stand shoulder to shoulder, they make a wall of defense against the enemy. This shield for front-line battle was not the little round shield they wore over one arm for hand to hand combat; it was a great big shield of wood covered with metal or heavy leather that an entire body could hide behind. When arrows (temptations and trials) come at us from the Evil One, we will be safe if we are each covered with the shield of faith. If we have placed our lives in God's hands, we are each behind the shield, a place where we trust God entirely to keep us from evil. Bad things may happen, but they can't destroy us if we are living by faith.

Let's Talk:

Can you think of a time you needed a shield of faith against one of Satan's arrows, a temptation or a trial?

To Learn More:

For more insight into the battle we fight, read 1 Peter 5:8–9.

Prayer:

"Dear Lord, thank You for giving us faith, a faith that can protect us from all the fiery darts of temptation and trials that Satan may throw at us. Thank You for going with us into every battle. In Your name we pray, amen."

Devotion 56

Scripture:

In addition to all this, take up the shield of faith, with which you can extinguish all the flaming arrows of the evil one (Ephesians 6:16).

I want to spend another day on this verse so I can give you a first-hand example of how this worked for one of the children in our family. One day we were talking about some friends whose little girl had leukemia. We said we had better pray for her. Someone mentioned how hard it was for the family to have a child so sick and in the hospital so often. One of our other children then said, "Why do some people have such troubles when nothing bad has ever happened to us?" This question came from a kid whose father was killed and who himself came very close to death when hit by a car. He was in the hospital for six weeks and in a body cast at home for five weeks. And now he observed that "nothing bad ever happens to us"!?

Part of his response may have been his age—early teens often feel invincible. But I think that he had succeeded in looking at those trials as something other than "bad things." In filling his mind with promises from God's Word, in seeing what good he could learn from whatever trial he endured, those evil things had fallen off of him, like fiery darts bouncing off his shield of faith. They weren't easy things to live through. Those times were times of fighting against worry, fear, and pain. But the point is, he lived through them undamaged (though not unchanged). The shield of faith had protected his heart and soul from being destroyed by his trials.

Let's Talk:

Can you think of something that has hit your "shield of faith" but bounced off, leaving you possibly changed but not damaged?

To Learn More:

For further meditation, read 1 John 5:2–5.

Prayer:

"Thank You Father for going with us into battle. Thank You that no bad thing can destroy us if we put our lives into Your hands. Amen."

Devotion 57

Scripture:
Take the helmet of salvation and the sword of the Spirit, which is the word of God (Ephesians 6:17).

According to my Bible commentary, the verb *take* in this verse means "receive" or "accept." We accept salvation as a gift from God. Jesus Christ died to pay for the sins of all who believe. If we accept that Jesus died to take the penalty for our sins, then our salvation is sure. The sureness of our salvation goes with us, acting as protection for our heads. Like soldiers, our heads are one of the most important parts of our bodies needing preservation, for inside the head is the mind which controls all the actions. When our heads are full of the truth from God's Word, the truth of salvation, there will not be room for bad or fearful thoughts.

Let's Talk:
Have you ever thought about doing something bad? Maybe no one was looking, and you thought you could get away with it. But then you remembered what God did. He sent His Son, Jesus, to die for you. Does remembering that make you want to obey Him and do the right thing?

To Learn More:
For more on the war for our minds, read Romans 7:22–25.

Prayer:
"Dear Jesus, beginning with the truth of salvation, please help us to fill our minds with the truth from Your Word. We pray that truth will keep us from doing wrong. Thank You that Your Spirit does battle against evil with us, and that we are not in the fight alone. In Your name, amen."

See *Commentary of the Whole Bible*, ed. Jamieson, Fausset, and Brown (Grand Rapids: Zondervan Publishing House, 1976).

Devotion 58

Scripture:

Take the helmet of salvation and the sword of the Spirit, which is the word of God (Ephesians 6:17).

Yesterday we talked about taking up the helmet of salvation mentioned in the first part of this verse. Today we will talk about "the sword of the Spirit." When I was a young child in Sunday school we would have what we called "Sword drills." The leader would call out a certain Scripture reference. We would look it up as quickly as we could, stand, and read the verse. We said we were "sharpening our swords for battle," the idea being that the more familiar we are with God's Word, the easier it will be to battle evil. If our minds are full of God's Word, we will be sharp, ready to defend ourselves, not only against temptations but against wrong teachings.

Let's Talk:

Have you ever been tempted to think that nothing good could possibly come out of the pain you have because your parent went away? Have you had the experience of filling your mind with God's Word and of feeling your whole outlook change?

To Learn More:

To see how Jesus used the Word of God against sin, read about His temptation in Matthew 4:1–11.

Prayer:

"Dear Father God, give us the mind of Christ that we may see what You want us to see in all our pain and trials. Thank You for Your Word. Help us to use it to think the way You want us to think. In Jesus' name and for Your glory we pray. Amen."

Devotion 59

Scripture:

And pray in the Spirit on all occasions with all kinds of prayers and requests (Ephesians 6:18).

We have talked a lot about the armor of God and how putting it on protects us from doing evil as well as from the evil things that may happen to us. The verse we just read comes right after the verses about the armor. We are told to pray on every occasion with all kinds of prayers and requests. Colossians 4:2 says to "devote yourselves to prayer, being watchful and thankful." It, like the verse above, reminds us that whenever we have an opportunity, we should praise and thank God.

We also need to come to God with all our burdens and requests. Not only will we begin to feel better for having shared the burden, we will feel the presence of God. As time goes on, we will see the answers to our prayers and will know even more how faithful He is. God's power is released in our lives through prayer. We feel His presence when we pray. All of this is a reminder of how important prayer is in addition to putting on the whole armor of God.

Let's Talk:

Is there a time you felt better after praying or that you felt God's presence? Or do you have an answer to prayer you'd like to tell us about?

To Learn More:

For more on the effectiveness of prayer, read Luke 11:1–12.

Prayer:

"Dear Lord, help us to be faithful every day in putting on the truth, righteousness, and the gospel. May we always be protected by our faith, and keep us faithful in prayer that we may stand against all kinds of evil. Thank You that You are greater than any evil in the world around us. In the great and mighty name of Jesus we pray, amen."

Devotion 60

Scripture:

If we are faithless, he will remain faithful, for he cannot disown himself (2 Timothy 2:13).

In this battle of good and evil that we have been talking about, we each have a part. We can put on the full armor of God and stand firm against the Devil. We can choose not to listen to our evil desires and not to sin. But we are not perfect. Sometimes there is a crack in the armor. We let negative or evil thinking from the world around us into our thoughts and actions. Sometimes we get angry with the way things are going, sometimes we get angry with God. But this verse is so special. It tells us that even when our faith is low, when we have not chosen the good, even when we are tempted to not trust Him, and certainly to not obey Him, He is still faithful! He is there. When we are ready to turn back to obedience, He is there. When we seek Him, putting aside our sin, we will find Him, for He always remains faithful.

Let's Talk:

What are the times we are most likely to get angry at the way things are going or angry at God? When do you *not* wear your full armor against the Devil?

To Learn More:

For more on the faithfulness of God, read Hebrews 6:17–19.

Prayer:

"Dear Father, thank You that You are ever faithful. Help us to be faithful to You. Help us to love You, obey You, and never stop trusting that You know what You are doing with our lives. In Jesus' name, amen."

Devotion 61

Scripture:

The secret things belong to the Lord our God (Deuteronomy 29:29).

We have talked a lot about why bad things may happen to us, how we can respond when they do, and what God is doing in us and for us. But when it comes right down to it, there are many things that we simply do not and will not ever know or understand. When I see God at work in my life, when I feel His presence, when I see my children grow into fine young people despite all that has happened to them, I can believe that God is at work in my life. But when my friend gets an incurable disease, when little children are abused and I read about it in the paper, when evil is all around me, sometimes I feel really angry and say, "Where is God in this!?" But the truth is, I don't know. I only know what He is doing in my life and, on a certain level, in the lives of those close to me. I cannot know and understand for everyone else. This is where I must trust Him. I shouldn't be angry about someone else's circumstances, because I don't know what God is doing over there or around the world. The unknown things are known only to Him.

Let's Talk:

What are some situations you know about where you are wondering how God is working there? Can you trust Him when you don't understand?

To Learn More:

For further meditation, read Romans 11:33–36.

Prayer:

"Dear Jesus, forgive me for getting angry with You. I realize from this verse that I cannot know and understand everything. There are many things that are secrets, known only to You. Help my faith to be big enough to trust You anyway. In Your name, amen."

Devotion 62

Scripture:

"Come to me, all you who are weary and burdened, and I will give you rest" (Matthew 11:28).

One morning while waiting for the bus, Andrew decided to practice his golf swing. He swung his club a few times and about the third time or so, he decided to really swing it hard. Believe it or not, on the back-swing the club went flying through the air! It ricocheted off the top of the open garage door, came down at a freaky angle inside the garage, and crashed neatly through the rear window of his father's car. The car was covered up for the winter. It was possible that his dad wouldn't even see the hole in the window for weeks or maybe even months. Andrew went to school.

That day he had two tests. But he couldn't concentrate at all. His mind was burdened with his unconfessed guilt. He failed one test and did very poorly on the other. Andrew's problem got so big inside of him that he couldn't eat much lunch, and by supper time, he was so burdened he could hardly eat at all. Finally, he said, "Mom and Dad, can I see you out in the garage?" There he told us what happened, and showed us the hole. His burden was lifted because he confessed what he had done, but then he was scared. What would his father do?

Because Andrew was responsible, he had to help pay for the window. But there was really no punishment. When his father told him there was no punishment, his burden was lifted. He ate a huge bed-time snack and slept very well that night. Andrew had peace and rest when he confessed. His dad had to spend a Saturday morning putting in the new glass.

Jesus says, Come to Me with your burdens. I have already taken your punishment. You may have to live with some responsibility for past deeds, but you won't be punished with eternal damnation because I have taken the punishment for you. Because I paid for your sins, you don't have to be afraid of God our Father, and you don't have to live with a terrible burden inside of you.

Let's Talk:

Do you have a story like Andrew's to tell? What happened?

To Learn More:

For further assurance, read Psalm 55:22.

Prayer:

"Dear Jesus, thank You for paying for our sins. Help us to bring all our burdens to You. Amen."

Devotion 63

Scripture:

For we are God's workmanship, created in Christ Jesus to do good works (Ephesians 2:10).

Not all families are blended because of a parent going away and the mom or dad getting married again. Some families are blended because they have adopted children. In a family that we know, both of the parents have white skin, some of the children have white skin, some have brown skin, and some are darker still. When the mom of this family found out she was going to give birth to a child, one of the children excitedly asked, "I wonder if this baby will be black, white, or brown!"

In the language in which the book of Ephesians was originally written, the word *workmanship* gave the idea of a "work of art." We are all special "works of art," created by God to love Him and serve Him. How we look doesn't matter. It's what's in our hearts that counts. Do we have hearts that want to do good for God?

Each of you is very special, created by God to do something special for Him. Not everyone looks the same, and not everyone is good at doing the same sorts of things. Some of the children in our family are good at being in front of an audience, some are not. Some of our children read like a whiz, understanding difficult words, while some are better in math. Some of our children love art and music, and some love sports. The important thing is to use whatever we are good at for God. Sometimes we have to think about how to do that. But we have all been created differently in order to do good works for God.

Let's Talk:

What are you good at? How can you use your talents for God?

To Learn More:

To learn more about the creation of all people, read Genesis 2.

Prayer:

"Dear Lord, thank You for making each person different. Help us to use our uniqueness to do good works for You. In Jesus' name, amen."

Devotion 64

Scripture:

"No eye has seen, no ear has heard, no mind has conceived what God has prepared for those who love him" (1 Corinthians 2:9).

Yesterday we talked about how God made each person different, a unique "work of art." This verse says that God has a plan for His children that is so awesome that no one has ever seen or heard nor can anyone's mind even envision how wonderful the plan is. But there is a condition on the truth of God's having a plan. The verse says, "for those who love him."

When my children lost their father, it was really tough to believe that any kind of plan was going on, much less a good plan. The girl's mother died because of cancer. How could that be part of a plan? The boy's father was killed when someone decided to drive drunk; how can that be part of a good plan? Maybe your parent left for reasons that just don't seem right or fair to you. How can that be part of any kind of plan? But this verse assures us that IF you love God, He DOES have a plan. Our families had so much hope that a wonderful plan had been made for us because we know that our loved ones loved God, and we love God too. This scripture reminds us that if we let Him have our life, He can give it a program that is so great and awesome that our minds cannot comprehend it.

Let's Talk:

What are some plans you think God might have for your life?

To Learn More:

For further meditation, read 1 Corinthians 2:6–16.

Prayer:

"Dear Jesus, thank You that nothing happens by accident if we love You. Help us to love You and to be willing let You work out the great plan that You have for our lives. In Jesus' name, amen."

Devotion 65

. . . .

Scripture:

For who is God besides the Lord? And who is the Rock except our God? He makes my feet like the feet of a deer; he enables me to stand on the heights (Psalm 18:31, 33).

In Michigan we often see deer, startled by headlights, run in great leaps and bounds across country roads. Sometimes, usually in fall and spring, we see them in groups grazing on the stubble of fields. When we see them run, we recognize them as some of the most graceful of all hoofed animals. God created the deer with a split hoof that acts like two toes, making them extremely sure-footed. Mountain deer, with the same confident leaps and bounds, are able to quickly scale the side of the steepest slopes. When taking a stand on solid rock, they can fight off enemies with their strong antlers and sharp front hoofs as weapons. But usually, because they are so swift and sure-footed, they prefer to run away.

When you are tempted to do something wrong, you can think of it as an attack by "the enemy." This passage says that God will help you be as sure-footed as a deer. You may "flee from evil" or, if necessary, God will be like the solid rock on which you can stand firm and fight.

When you are facing a difficult situation, you may feel like you are up against a sheer mountain wall with no way around or over. But God promises to make you as agile and swift as a deer. With feet like a deer, you can scale the steepest mountain!

Let's Talk:

Have you ever felt like you were in a "no win" situation, and when you stepped out, trusting in God, He got you over it, one step at a time? Let's share those kinds of times with each other. Or, if you are facing a tough time right now, let's pray and ask God to give us "feet like the feet of a deer."

To Learn More:

Hebrews 2:18 and 1 Corinthians 13 offer further promises of escape from temptation.

. . . .

Prayer:

"Dear God, please give us feet as swift as deer, to run away from evil. And when our lives seem as difficult to live as scaling a mountain, give us agility and strength to climb up and over our problems. In Jesus' name, amen."

Devotion 66

Scripture:
"And lead us not into temptation, but deliver us from the evil one"
(Matthew 6:13).

Yesterday we talked about how God gives His children feet like deer to flee temptation. This verse tells us that we can ask God to protect us from temptation before it happens. To ask to be protected from the enticement of evil is a very practical and protective thing to ask. We may think about praying for help when we are faced with tough choices, but it's great to know that we can pray to keep the temptation away, too! In the world many things will entice us, but we can ask Jesus to help us not to be tempted. If we know we are going to face temptation at school or work tomorrow, we can ask Jesus ahead of time to deliver us. This is similar to the idea of putting on the full armor of God that we discussed before.

Making a decision ahead of time is often the best protection one can have. If you know you may be in a situation where others will pressure you to smoke, to try a drug, to cheat, or to participate in any destructive behavior, you can decide ahead of time to say NO. You can ask God ahead of time to make you strong in the face of attractions that are hard for you to say no to.

Let's Talk:
Perhaps none of the things I mentioned are difficult for you to say no to. But you can probably think of some things that *are* appealing to you that you know you shouldn't do. Share them with your family, and you can all pray together that you will not be lead into temptation but delivered from evil.

To Learn More:
2 Peter 2:9 and 1 John 4:4 are more helpful verses about how God's power is greater than our temptations.

Prayer:
"Dear Father, protect us from evil. Thank You. Amen."

Devotion 67

Scripture:

"Forgive us our debts, as we also have forgiven our debtors" (Matthew 6:12).

This verse, as well as the verse we read yesterday, are taken from a prayer that Jesus prayed when He was teaching His disciples to pray. It is usually called, "The Lord's Prayer." We can learn many things from this prayer. Besides teaching His followers to ask for protection from evil, He taught them to ask for forgiveness of their sins and to forgive others. (The word *debts* means "sin.") If we want Jesus to forgive our sins, we need to forgive others the wrongs that they have done to us. In fact, after the end of His prayer, Jesus amplifies this point and tells His disciples, "if you do not forgive other people their sins, your Father will not forgive your sins" (verse 15). Yikes! How can this be? We have said before that forgiveness for sins is a free gift that we accept from God by believing that His Son died for us. This looks like there is a condition on our forgiveness.

Remember though, this was a lesson Jesus was giving to those who were already His disciples. If we are His children, and His spirit lives within us, we are in the process of becoming more like Him. That means we will become forgiving in the way that He is forgiving. God the Father wants to see His character reflected in His children. As His children, to ask Him for forgiveness when we refuse to forgive others is to repress His Spirit within us.

Let's Talk:

What are some things we need to forgive other people for? Have you ever forgiven somebody when it was hard, but afterwards you were so glad you did?

To Learn More:

For more about this, read the story in Matthew 18:21–35.

Prayer:

"Dear Jesus, help us, with Your power and Your love, to forgive others the wrongs that they do to us. Please make us more and more like You. In Your name, amen."

Devotion 68

. . . .

Scripture:

Be kind and compassionate to one another, forgiving each other, just as in Christ God forgave you (Ephesians 4:32).

"I never want to be friends with Janey again. All she ever does is criticize me and tell me what to do!" Susan cried.

"What did she actually do?" asked her mother.

"Well, it's hard to explain," Susan went on. "Like, we'll just be playing along and all of a sudden she'll say something really mean, like 'Move your fat caboose out of my way,' or 'Your hair is ugly, I could fix it if you want.' It's as if she doesn't even think she's being mean, but she is."

Mother felt sad for her daughter's hurt feelings. She said, "We know that you aren't fat. And I think your hair looks very nice. Perhaps Janey doesn't realize she's hurting your feelings. Maybe next time she says something hurtful, you should tell her right away how it makes you feel."

"I tried that. She just gets mad and huffs off. I feel like I have to be nice all the time to keep peace, but she can say or do whatever she wants," Susan explained.

Her mother thought a minute. Then she said, "You know, honey, you don't have to be friends with her. If she really makes you miserable, you don't have to play together, but you do have to forgive her."

"Forgive her! I don't see why I should. She never says she's sorry. She never thinks she's wrong! Why should I forgive her?"

"You have to forgive her because Jesus forgives you," explained her mother. "He forgives you for all your sins, even the ones you haven't committed yet." (Romans 5:6) "Remember the place in the Lord's Prayer where it says, 'Forgive us our debts as we forgive our debtors'? God forgives us, but He says He'll not forgive His children who don't forgive others. Let's pray together and ask Jesus to help you forgive."

Let's Talk:

Have you ever had a difficult friend? Do you think you can forgive him or her?

. . . .

Devotions for the Blended Family

To Learn More:

Read Matthew 18:21–35 for a parable on forgiveness.

Prayer:

"Dear Lord Jesus, help us to use Your love and strength within us to forgive others. In Your name, amen."

Devotion 69

Scripture:

Worship the LORD with gladness (Psalm 100:2).

Whatever you do, work at it with all your heart, as working for the Lord (Colossians 3:23).

Mother had an agreement with one of the children that he/she would be a summer helper. Mom wanted to work on a special project and thought if one of the kids who needed some money wanted to do extra work beyond his/her routine chores, she would pay him/her, and it would be a convenient arrangement for both. But it wasn't a good idea. The child who agreed to be the helper seldom did the job without reminders and would often quit before the job was done. When Mother had to keep checking on the child's progress or finish the job herself, the "help" was of little value.

Did you know that what you do for others you are doing for Jesus? Mom and Dad can do their job to the glory of God, and kids who help their parents are serving the Lord, too, if they serve with gladness. Our attitudes make all the difference in whether or not we are doing our work for the Lord.

Let's Talk:

Can you think of ways to serve God by helping at home? If you have a bad attitude, what kind of thoughts will help you to change your attitude?

To Learn More:

For more instruction on how to serve Christ, read Romans 12:9–21.

Prayer:

"Dear Lord, help us to do all things as if we are doing them for You in person. Thank You that we can do all things through Christ who gives us strength. In Jesus' name, amen."

Devotion 70

Scripture:

Giving thanks always for all things (Ephesians 5:20 KJV).

"I'm sick of making my bed; I don't have to make it at my dad's house," grumbled Kevin. "And why do I have to pick up my clothes every day? It really interferes with my time."

Mom's answer may have been a little preachy, but she reminded Kevin, "God wants us to give thanks for all things."

"You mean, I should thank God for having to pick up my clothes and make my bed? I can't feel thankful for having to do work!" Kevin exclaimed.

"Well," said Mother, "there are people in the world who are so poor they don't have a nice warm bed. Many people sleep right on the floor or have just one blanket. And you know that many kids don't have the amount of nice clothes that you have."

"So you mean that when I make my bed or pick up my clothes, I should thank God that I have a nice warm bed and so many nice clothes?" asked Kevin.

"Yup," said Mom. "And most of what we have is like that. God has given us so many material blessings, we need to be good caretakers of what He has given. Our houses and cars and clothes and even the very earth are all gifts from God. We please Him and show Him appreciation when we take good care of His gifts. And for you to pick up your clothes and make your bed is just the beginning of teaching you to be a good caretaker of God's gifts."

Let's Talk:

How do you show your appreciation for your blessings? Do you feel that Mom and Dad are mean or unfair when they ask you to take care of your things or ask you to help out? How can you change your attitude?

To Learn More:

Colossians 3:15–17 tells us more about the gratitude we should have in our hearts toward God.

Prayer:

"Dear Lord, help us to take good care of what You have given us. In Jesus' name, amen."

Devotion 71

Scripture:

Even a child is known by his actions, by whether his conduct is pure and right (Proverbs 20:11).

There have been times when I have said to my children, Today I talked to Mrs. So and So. She's so nice. It would be fun for me if you were friends with her children. Sometimes they say, Oh, we don't have anything in common, or I guess it could happen. But a few times they have answered, I can't believe you want me to be friends with them. They get drunk every weekend, or they sleep with their dates and don't even try to obey God's law about chastity. Sometimes the answer is more vague, like, They hang around with a rough crowd that swears a lot and talks mean to each other, I just wouldn't feel comfortable with them. The observations that my children have made remind me of this verse. No matter how young or old we are, we are known by our behavior. We all make mistakes sometimes, we are not perfectly good all the time. Then we hope that others will forgive us just as we forgive them. But as we live and grow in one place, we become known by how we behave. It's easy to say that we are Christians, but people can tell whether we really love Jesus by the way that we act.

Let's Talk:

What have you done this week that would show others that you love God? What have you done that would make others wonder if you do or not? Remember, if we confess our sins, he will forgive us our sins (1 John 1:9).

To Learn More:

For further meditation, read Matthew 7:15–21.

Prayer:

"Dear Lord, help us to consistently act like persons who love You. For Your glory we pray. Amen."

Devotion 72

. . . .

Scripture:

We ought always to thank God for you, brothers, and rightly so, because your faith is growing more and more, and the love every one of you has for each other is increasing (2 Thessalonians 1:3).

First you were a little baby. Then you grew. When we first got married, we felt love for one another, but it was sort of a "baby" love. As time goes on and we go through more experiences together, we can feel our love growing. We may have had moments of frustration and of feeling overwhelmed when we thought, *What have I gotten myself into?* But as we renew our commitment each day, continue to make memories, and experience the ups and downs of life together, our love grows.

This verse says that our faith grows, too. When we first give our lives to Jesus, we believe that He died for us, and maybe that is just about all we know. Maybe, when we first entered God's family, all we felt was relief or gratitude that our sins are forgiven. But as we live more and more of our lives as His children and we begin to see the plans unfold that He has for us, when we feel Him near in tough times, when His Word speaks to us with the wisdom we have been needing, all of these things make us grow in faith. As our faith gets bigger, our love for God grows bigger.

Let's Talk:

Can you think of the many things that you have learned and how you've changed as you've grown? Do you remember when your mom or dad first got married again and how you misunderstood things about each other that now you understand? Can you think of how you have grown in faith? Have you learned to know Jesus better?

To Learn More:

For further meditation, read 1 John 4:7–12. It has a lot to say about the growing love we can have for one another.

Prayer:

"Dear Jesus, help us to grow in faith and in love every day. Thank You. Amen."

. . . .

Devotion 73

Scripture:

Since God so loved us, we also ought to love one another (1 John 4:11).

For God hath not given us the spirit of fear; but of power, and of love . . . (2 Timothy 1:7 KJV).

Sometimes the hardest people to love are the ones we live with. When we are feeling angry with ourselves or have hurt feelings, or sometimes just because we're tired and under stress, we don't treat each other very nicely. Sometimes when we are angry with the parent who left, we take it out on the parent who is there. Sometimes we fight with our brothers or sisters just because we're sick of them always being there and of having to share space and attention with them. This verse tells us that if we love God, then we ought to love one another. It's not always easy. But remember, God puts His Spirit in His children, and if we ask Him, He will give us the power to love one another. I don't think we can love each other without His help.

Let's Talk:

When is it difficult for you to love the members of your family? Is there something each of you can do to make it easier for others to love you?

To Learn More:

For more on love, read 1 John 4:16–21.

Prayer:

"Dear Jesus, fill us with Your love and power every day. Help us to use Your love and power to love one another. In Your name we pray, amen."

Devotion 74

Scripture:

Call to me and I will answer you (Jeremiah 33:3).

I am your God . . . I will . . . help you (Isaiah 41:10).

Lisa and Mom had gone to the mall. Lisa was old enough to go to the music store alone while Mom parked the car and went to the dress shop. After picking out her sheet music, Lisa was supposed to meet Mom at the dress shop. But there was a big recreational vehicle show going on at the mall that weekend, and everything looked different. All the campers and trailers filled up the usual open spaces, and Lisa felt confused. She went in the direction she knew the dress shop would be and thought she found the right place. She kept going in and out of the same shop, sure it was the right one, but Mom wasn't there.

There are several places at the mall to ask for directions, and of course any salesperson in any shop will gladly help, but Lisa was afraid to ask. They all seemed busy, and she felt like a bother, and maybe she was a little afraid. Finally, she did ask the saleswoman, "Is this the dress shop?"

"No," the woman smiled, "this is the maternity shop. The dress shop is next door."

Mom was waiting in the dress shop just like she said she would be. And she was talking with the saleswoman there about how to get help to look for Lisa!

Let's Talk:

Have you ever been afraid to "bother" God? How big do you think your trouble has to be before you can ask God for help? Some people think that God may be too busy or may not care about the "little things." But just the opposite is true. God wants His children to come to Him all the time, any time, with any request.

To Learn More:

For further meditation, read Isaiah 41:9–13.

Prayer:

"Dear Lord, thank You for always being there for us. Thank You for helping us when we come to You. In Jesus' name, amen."

Devotion 75

Scripture:

Do not merely listen to the word . . . Do what it says (James 1:22).

If you love me, you will obey what I command (John 14:15).

In the Bible we learn the good news that God loves us, that Jesus died for us, and that God wants us to be His children. But the Bible is also a guide book for living. In it God tells us what He expects of us in relationship to Him and in our relationships to one another. In these verses, James and John are reminding us that we need to obey God. Since He is our Creator, He knows what works for us. The guidelines for living found in His Word are things that will help us to get along better with Him and with others. If we love Him, we will want to do what His Word says.

Over the next few days we will talk about God's moral laws. They are most often known as the Ten Commandments. Many things about the way of life in Bible times were different from how they are now. But God's moral law is unchanging. The commandments reflect the holiness of God and are a perfect standard of behavior.

Let's Talk:

Can you think of a time when a relationship with someone in your family improved when you applied God's standards to your behavior? If not, hang on for the next few days. You may begin to see what God has in mind for our behavior in relationship to Himself and to others, and as you do what He says, maybe you will see changes.

To Learn More:

Read Luke 6:46–49 for an illustration of those who obey and those who do not obey what the Word of the Lord says.

Prayer:

"Dear Father God, thank You that You gave us guidelines for living that are unchangeable. Help us to love You and to obey You. In Jesus' name and by the power of Your Spirit we pray, amen."

Devotion 76

. . . .

Scripture:

You shall have no other gods before me. You shall not make for yourself an idol in the form of anything in heaven above or on the earth beneath or in the waters below. You shall not bow down to them or worship them (Deuteronomy 5:7–9).

The first four commandments comprise our duties to God—the other six, our duties to those around us. These verses are the first two of the commandments—to have no God other than the God of the Bible and not to worship any idol. It is not too difficult to understand what this means. The God of the Bible is the only God, and He demands our complete loyalty. You cannot be a Christian and be a worshiper of another god or be involved in another religion at the same time.

At the time of the Old Testament, many people worshiped idols. That means that they would pray, praise, and sacrifice to statues. This is not common in the United States, though it does occur. God says we must not be involved in idol worship. But there is another way to "worship" an "idol." If *anything* in our lives is more important than God, then we are worshiping idols.

Think about the following questions and answer them silently in your heart. What do you think about the most? Who do you worry about pleasing the most? Is it God? What do you spend every free minute filling your mind with? Is it the music you hear on the radio; is it the messages on the TV? Or is it the truth about God? What about hobbies? Do you play video games or golf every spare minute but never have time to read God's Word or to pray? Search your mind and heart. Whatever you emphasize the most in your life could be your idol. Do you really worship God above all gods?

Let's Talk:

Let's go over again some common things people like us often worship more than God Himself.

To Learn More:

To read the story of what happened to the Israelites when they worshiped an idol, read Exodus 32.

Prayer:

"Dear Lord, help us to put You first, above all else. Amen."

. . . .

Devotion 77

Scripture:

You shall not misuse the name of the LORD your God, for the LORD will not hold anyone guiltless who misuses his name (Deuteronomy 5:11).

In Old Testament times, the name of Jehovah God was so sacred and holy that God's people would not speak His name out loud. It was represented in the Hebrew Scriptures by the letters *YHWH*. When they had to talk about God, they would just say the name LORD. In these days, people not only do not hold the name of God as sacred, they often misuse it. God cares about the way we treat His name, because it is an indication of how we feel toward Him in our hearts.

How does a person misuse the name of God? To use God's name in a derogatory or careless manner, in a way that dishonors rather than honors Him, is to misuse His name. You can think of many examples of this in almost every movie and on many T.V. shows when the actors use the name of God in a careless way. Is it hard for you to not do as those around you and use the name of God carelessly?

Remember, this is serious to God, important enough to be part of His permanent moral law. The way we use God's name shows how we feel in our hearts towards Him.

Let's Talk:

Can we help one another be more careful in this area? How?

To Learn More:

For a New Testament slant on this commandment, read Ephesians 4:25–33, especially verse 29.

Prayer:

"Dear Father God, please forgive us if we have ever used Your name carelessly. Help us to honor You by keeping Your name sacred. In Jesus' name, amen."

Devotion 78

Scripture:

Observe the Sabbath day by keeping it holy (Deuteronomy 5:12).

God made a special day for His people to rest from their labors and to take time to worship Him together. Did you know that the idea of a day of rest did not begin with the Law but with God at creation? Genesis 2:2 tells how God rested from His labors of creation and blessed that day of rest. The people of the Old Testament referred to this day as the Sabbath. Most of the Christians in our culture celebrate the Sabbath on Sunday. On this day we make a point of only doing work that is necessary and works that help others, like visiting shut-ins and caring for the sick.

When we first got married, our children were very busy with friends and could go many days without playing together at all. So, to make the Lord's Day special for us, on Sunday we only spend time with each other and don't have other kids over to play. It's not wrong for people to play with their friends on Sunday—this is just one of the ways our family chose to make the day more restful and different from the rest of the week. First we spend time with God when we go to church as a family. Then we continue our "rest" (our break from the usual routine) by spending time with each other.

Let's Talk:

Do you have a way of making the Lord's Day special? If not, can you think of a way to make it special? If Sunday is a day that you sometimes spend with one parent and then the other, you could make it special in a different way at each house.

To Learn More:

To read the specifics of this law of God, read Deuteronomy 5:12–15

Prayer:

"Dear Father God, help us to honor You by honoring Your day. Help us to keep it a special day. For Your glory we pray. Amen."

Devotion 79

Scripture:

I was glad when they said unto me, "Let us go to the house of the Lord" (Psalm 122:1 KJV).

"I don't see why I have to go to church!" Lori stormed. "I never have to go when I'm at my mom's house. I don't have any friends to hang around with there. What's the big deal any way?"

"Lori," said her father, "I wish you had friends here, too. Maybe when you have visited often enough you will. But friends are not really the reason why we go to God's house. We go to church to worship and praise God and to learn more about His Word."

"Perhaps," her father continued, "if you try to participate in the singing and you really listen to what the pastor says, maybe the time will go faster and it won't seem so bad then. Sometimes taking notes or drawing pictures of what is being said will help you listen and give you something to do. Maybe if you go with an attitude of seeing just how much you can participate, you'll get a lot more out of it. Come on, try. And we can even pray that you'll feel better about it today."

Let's Talk:

What would you tell Lori? Can a kid worship and praise God? How? Do you think that if Lori tries to obey her dad and participates in worship that she may feel differently about it?

To Learn More:

For an experience of praise and worship at home, read 1 Chronicles 16:23–36.

Prayer:

"Dear Father in heaven, help us to be glad to come to Your house. Help us to be able to stop thinking about ourselves and to concentrate on You and to worship You. May we remember what Jesus has done for us. With grateful hearts, bring us to worship. For Your glory and in Your Son's name we pray, amen."

Devotion 80

Scripture:
Honor your father and your mother (Deuteronomy 5:16).

"My mom never did it that way! Why do you? Why should I do what *you* want?" Tammy wailed as she ran to her room, threw herself on her bed, and cried.

This was a tough moment for me as a stepmom. I cried a little, too. And I asked God to help me. Then I went in and talked to Tammy. I told her that I knew I was not her "real" mom and that I would not ever try to take her mother's place. But I am the mom that is here in this house. Her father and I were trying to do what we believed to be the best, and when he wasn't there, I had to be the parent.

Through much talking and praying together and even some counseling, Tammy and all of our children have learned how to honor not only their birth parents but their stepparents as well. But what does *honor* mean?

My dictionary lists words such as: *respect, regard,* and *credit* for the meaning of honor. We as parents and stepparents do many things to care for our children. As a stay-at-home mom in the past, I am the one who has shopped for food and clothing, cooked, done laundry, and taken care of those who are sick, for both birth children and stepchildren equally. Dad works to support our family and also spends a lot of time on upkeep for our house and lawn and cars. He fixes things for all of us. Both Dad and I are the ones who talk over our children's problems with them and try very hard, working together, to solve the issues of our family. Most of all, we give a lot of thought and a lot of time to teaching our children not only right and wrong but skills for living. We do not do any of these things perfectly. And we often make mistakes. But all of the things we do for you, this verse says, makes us deserve the credit, the honor, for doing them.

Your parents may divide up the jobs of family living differently than we do at our house, but regardless of the jobs they do to raise you, they are the ones who parent you and care for you and teach you how to live. For this they should be given credit and respect.

Answer these questions to yourself. Do you honor your parents? That means, do you treat them with respect and give them credit for all they do for you? Remember, you can ask God to help you obey Him.

Let's Talk:

What are the "mom" jobs at your house? What are the "dad" jobs? What do they both do to raise you and care for you and teach you how to live?

To Learn More:

Read the entire verse of Deuteronomy 5:16 to learn the blessing you will get for honoring your parents.

Prayer:

"Dear Jesus, please send Your healing, strengthening Spirit to us, so that we may honor our parents. In Your name we pray, amen."

Devotion 81

. . . .

Scripture:

You shall not murder (Deuteronomy 5:17).

But I tell you that any one who is angry with his brother will be subject to judgment (Matthew 5:22).

Many urban middle school children in America recently participated in a poll on violence. A very large percentage of them said they thought it was okay to shoot someone who had stolen from them. It was not clear whether these kids understood that shooting would do harm or possibly kill. In our culture we watch so much television and see so many movies where people get shot but it doesn't matter that it seems we have forgotten how valuable human life is. When someone uses a gun to "punish" another, that person may very well die. When people die, they are *dead*; their physical lives are over. God says in His law that it is wrong to take another person's life.

You may say, "I'd never shoot someone. We don't even have guns where I live!" That may be true. But have you ever thought of how you "kill" someone's spirit when you "shoot" a person with mean words? We can be very destructive to a person's spirit when we make fun of him or her or talk in a mean way. Think about "you shall not commit murder" in terms of "murdering" a person's spirit or hurting his or her feelings. Then you may find that this law of God really does apply to you.

Let's Talk:

What are some ways we kill another person's spirit or hurt his or her feelings? Have you ever felt someone "shoot" at your feelings?

To Learn More:

To read more of Jesus' teaching on angry words being like murder, read all of Matthew 5:21–22. For God's principles of self-defense and His response to murder and accidental murder, you may want to read Numbers 35:6–33.

Prayer:

"Dear Jesus, please forgive us for the times we have been hurtful and mean. Help us not to kill with words or with weapons. In Your name, amen."

. . . .

Devotion 82

Scripture:

You shall not commit adultery (Deuteronomy 5:18).

God made men and women to desire one another. In the Garden of Eden He brought Adam and Eve together and told them to "be fruitful and multiply" (Genesis 1:28) and also that married people are "one flesh" (Genesis 2:24). In the New Testament, the apostle Paul reminds the people of the Corinthian church not to withhold physical love from their marriage partners without an understanding because it may cause them to sin (1 Corinthians 4–5).

The sin he was talking about is *adultery*—to have sex with someone to whom you are not married. These passages of Scripture as well as others like the Song of Solomon show us that sex is a wonderful gift from God, designed to express married love and bind a man and a woman together. But a physical relationship outside of marriage is the opposite of what God wants for us. Instead of an expression of committed love and oneness of life, it is an act of selfish desire. According to Jesus in the New Testament, sex outside of marriage is sin against God, against self, and against others. Not only does it violate God's design, it is a dangerous risk for disease, even death from diseases like AIDS. But one of the most destructive things that adultery can do is cause divorce.

Many of the people reading this book will have experienced this pain. When the marriage promise "to stay faithful and cleave only onto thee" is not kept, hearts are broken and the entire family may be split apart. But adultery is not different from other sins in that God forgives anyone who confesses it and repents. Do you remember what these words mean? To *confess* means that we agree with God that we are wrong and we admit it to Him. *Repentance* means that we turn from our selfish ways and begin to live lives centered on God and what He wants. (You may want to go back and look at Devotion 16.) A person who has sex outside of marriage may have to suffer the consequences, like unwanted pregnancy, disease, or divorce. But God still gives forgiveness to all those who ask to receive it (1 John 1:9).

Let's Talk:

Let's review all the problems we avoid when we obey this commandment. Let's name again all the good things God gives us when we obey this commandment.

To Learn More:

For the apostle Paul's teachings on this subject, you may want to read 1 Corinthians 6:13–18 and 1 Corinthians 7:1–7.

Prayer:

"Dear Father, thank You for Your special plan for sex. Help us to obey it. Thank You for forgiving and loving us. In Jesus' name, amen."

Devotion 83

Scripture:
You shall not steal (Deuteronomy 5:19).

One day after shopping, Mom noticed that pre-school Andrew had a package of all-natural Life Savers in his pocket. She knew she had not purchased them, and he was too young to buy anything. She gave Andrew a serious talk about never taking anything from the store without paying for it. Then she drove back to the health food store and made him return the unopened package to the person behind the counter. He cried and cried from the embarrassment, but he still had to give it back and say "I'm sorry."

One day Tammy and Becky were playing on the floor. Tammy noticed something under Becky's bed and pulled out a stuffed mouse that she had never seen before. She took it to her mother. Mother talked to Becky and found out she had taken it from the gift shop, hiding it in her coat pocket and later, under her bed. Mother made her take it back, and she too, had to apologize.

A woman on a TV sitcom had just returned from the grocery store and noticed her son eating jelly beans. When she asked him where he got them, he said from the bulk-food container in the store. She yelled at him and told him never to take things without paying for them. "But," he said, "you go through the store eating things from the bulk-food containers." She answered, "It's only stealing when you leave the store with the stuff."

These stories may seem "cute" and "typical." But the truth is, God says in His unchanging moral law that it is wrong to take anything for yourself that does not belong to you. "You shall not steal" — period. The woman in the last story was teaching her child that it is okay to take "a little something" sometimes. But is it? What do you think?

Let's Talk:
Can you think of a time when you meant to "borrow" something and it turned out that you kept it? Is that stealing? What do you think?

To Learn More:

See also Exodus 22:1–15 to read more details about God's law to protect property. Ephesians 4:29 gives a New Testament slant to this law and advice for how to change.

Prayer:

"Dear Father, keep us from temptation. Help us to never take what is not ours. For Your glory we pray. Amen."

Devotion 84

Scripture:

You shall not give false testimony against your neighbor (Deuteronomy 5:20).

"Dad, I'm not sure, but I think I saw that stockclerk at the grocery store, the one named Craig, put some candy in his pocket while he worked," reported Matt hesitantly. "What should I do about it?"

While Dad and Matt discussed the problem, Cindi was listening. Before they even finished talking, she ran outside to play. There she and the neighbor girl began to talk. "Guess what I just heard?" said Cindi breathlessly.

"What?" said her friend.

"Craig at the grocery store was seen stealing candy!"

When her friend acted really interested and excited, Cindi decided to make the story even better. "He ate it right while he was working and pocketed some for later!"

"My! I wonder why he doesn't get fired?" puzzled the neighbor. That girl later told others, and soon very many people thought that Craig was a thief. The word got back to his employer, and he almost lost his job. He had to go on probation for awhile. And he had never stolen anything! Be very careful about what you say. And before you ever report on someone, make sure it is true and the person you are telling needs to know. If you know something bad, you don't need to tell it unless there is a specific reason, like to keep someone from harm or from harming others.

Words have the potential to damage someone, possibly ruin his or her life. So, to protect a person's reputation and good name, God says very specifically, "Do not say anything false against your neighbor."

Let's Talk:

What are some words and phrases you often hear about people that really hurt their reputations? What are some words and phrases we can use to silence our friends who might be spreading false rumors?

To Learn More:

Read Ephesians 4:25, which is a New Testament application of this law.

Prayer:

"Dear Jesus, please help us to never say anything untrue. Protect our tongues from evil, for our own good, the good of others, and for Your glory. In Jesus' name we pray, amen."

Devotion 85

Scripture:
You shall not covet (Deuteronomy 5:21).

This law of God is especially important because wanting what belongs to another leads to other sins. For example, I can't think of a case of theft where coveting did not precede the stealing. If I want my neighbor's wealth and I allow myself to continually dwell on what he or she has and I don't have, I am *coveting*. This obsession will at the very least lead to me feeling dissatisfied and unhappy all the time. At the very worst, it will lead to stealing. Think about the nature of robbery. Many murders are committed when people want to steal or to hide the fact that they have stolen. And the sin of adultery is also preceded by coveting. People will not take someone else's husband or wife if they have not first been thinking about and desiring what is not theirs. It was what they were thinking about first, the coveting, that led to the adultery. Coveting leads to many other sins, so God says, "Do not covet."

Let's Talk:
Can you think of a time when you really, really wanted to steal, but you didn't? Can you think of a time when you did take something that didn't belong to you? Can you remember the period of time you went through *before* the taking when you *just wanted to have it so bad*? That was the coveting stage. Can you think of a way that lying may be preceded by coveting?

To Learn More:
In Joshua 7:10–26, you can read a story about a person who coveted, then took something, and all of God's people suffered.

Prayer:
"Dear Heavenly Father, help us to be satisfied with all that You have given us. Help us not to excessively desire anything that You do not want us to have. In Jesus' name, amen."

Devotion 86

. . . .

Scripture:

. . . for he who loves his fellowman has fulfilled the law. The commandments, "Do not commit adultery," "Do not murder," "Do not steal," "Do not covet," and whatever other commandment there may be, are summed up in this one rule: "Love your neighbor as yourself" (Romans 13:8–9).

This verse is a good summary of what we have discussed the last few days. The ten commandments, also called God's moral law, are the guidelines we need in order to live the way God wants us to live, first in our relationship with Him and then in our relationships with others.

Some of God's laws may not be too difficult for you to keep. You probably don't worship idols; if your family goes to church regularly, then it may not be difficult at all to keep a special day holy to God. If no one in your family uses the name of God in a careless way, then you probably don't either. These are some of the laws concerning our relationship with God.

But often we have more trouble keeping the commandments that govern our relationships with other people. The verse above says that everything the law teaches about our relationships with others can be summed up in this one phrase: "Love your neighbor as yourself." Or, stated another way, "Do to others as you would have them do to you" (Luke 6:31). This has become known as "the Golden Rule." If we always abide by the idea of only doing to others what we would like them to do to us, we will fulfill the law perfectly.

Let's talk:

When you have a problem with someone, does it help if you remind yourself to do to them what you would want done to you? If you haven't tried it, do. Come back and share with your family how it went when you applied the Golden Rule.

To Learn More:

For further meditation, read Jesus' words in Luke 6:27–36.

Prayer:

"Dear Father in heaven, help us to treat others the way we would want to be treated. In Jesus' name, amen."

. . . .

Devotion 87

Scripture:

"I am the bread of life. He who comes to me will never go hungry, and he who believes in me will never be thirsty" (John 6:35).

Becky and Lisa raise gerbils. When they first began this venture, they read a book on the habits and care of gerbils and learned that these little creatures spend every twenty-four hours in cycles of rest and activity. But by watching them they learned something more. The gerbils' times of busyness are almost always preceded by eating. They need food to give them strength and energy for their times of activity.

When we want to obey God, when we try to serve God by serving others, when we do anything to live the Christian life, we need spiritual strength and energy. Remember many days back when we talked about the battle between good and evil and putting on the full armor of God? We will not have the energy or strength to fight the battle against the Evil One or against our temptations unless we have first eaten of the Bread of Life.

Jesus calls Himself the Bread of Life. We "eat" of Him when we fill our hearts and our minds with God's Word. Coming together with God's people on Sunday to worship and hear God's Word taught and having our own devotions at home are some of the ways that we eat and drink spiritually. These times with God "feed" us and give us strength and energy to do good, to be ready for spiritual activity.

Let's Talk:

Have you ever spent time with God, reading His Word and praying, and then immediately had to take a stand against doing wrong? Did having spent time eating "spiritual food" make it easier for you to stand against Satan?

To Learn More:

For more about spiritual eating and drinking, read 1 Peter 2:2 and Hebrews 5:12–14.

Prayer:

"Dear Father in heaven, help us to hunger and thirst after righteousness and to feed on Your Word. Thank You for Your Word that gives us strength and energy to battle evil and to do good. In Jesus' name, amen."

Devotion 88

Scripture:

Be kind and compassionate to one another (Ephesians 4:32).

Lisa was acting mad. When Mom asked her why, she said Andrew was being mean to her. "How is Andrew being mean to you?" Mother asked.

"Well, this morning when I was playing my video game," Lisa explained, "Andrew asked if he could play with me. I forced myself to say 'yes,' even though I really didn't want to, because I thought it was the nice thing to do. Now, I just asked him if I could play with him, and he said 'NO!' Andrew is mean. He isn't kind at all!"

"A-n-d-r-e-w," Mother called, "please come here."

Andrew came and sat down with Mom and Lisa. Mother asked Lisa to explain to him what happened and how she felt about it. Then Mother asked, "Andrew, why didn't you let Lisa play with you?"

Andrew thought a minute before answering, "I just didn't want to, and I didn't even think about it. I wasn't thinking about what was kind, I was just thinking about what I wanted to do."

Mother told him that he must learn to be kind and learn to think about others. Learning kindness would not only help him get along better with people but also is what pleases God. Then, because Andrew had not been sharing, Lisa got to play the video game for a whole hour by herself. They both decided during that hour that they would much rather be playing together and that when they thought of each other and were kind, it made the game better.

Let's Talk:

Can you think of a time when being kind ended up being more fun than just doing what you thought you wanted? Can you think of a time when you wished you had gotten your own way? Does it help when you think about the fact that it pleases God when you are kind?

To Learn More:

For further meditation, read 2 Peter 1:3–7.

Prayer:

"Dear Father in heaven, help us to be kind to one another, as You have been kind and forgiving to us. In Jesus' name we pray, amen."

Devotion 89

Scripture:

For he shall give his angels charge over thee, to keep thee in all thy ways (Psalm 91:11 KJV).

One day Aaron was riding his bike with friends. He had gotten out of the house a little behind them and was hurrying to catch up. Two of them crossed the street before he did. He looked as he came to the intersection, saw a car, and thought he could make it. He didn't. Although the driver swerved very hard, Aaron crashed into the side of his car. He had a broken leg and a skull-fracture. The lady in the corner house called an ambulance, and Aaron's friends told her how to call Aaron's dad at work. They gathered up his hat and bike and shoes and kept them for him. Another neighbor called Aaron's house and told the other kids not to worry and what to say to their mom when she got home from the store. The paramedics at the accident and, later, the emergency room staff at the hospital swarmed around Aaron to help him. When Mom got home from the store, she called Grandma and Grandpa, and they took the other kids out to eat while she went to the hospital.

All of these friends and neighbors and care-givers were like angels—there to help, comfort, and protect from further harm. But when Mom was finally alone with Aaron and she bent down to talk to him, he whispered to her, "Mom, the angels were there. They were all around." After a time, he forgot that he even said this. But Mom never forgot. God does send His angels to protect and comfort His people.

Let's Talk:

Have you ever had an experience like Aaron's, or has anyone ever told you about angels helping them?

To Learn More:

For further meditation, read all of Psalm 91.

Prayer:

"Dear Father, thank You that "our days are in Your hands." Thank You that the angels do watch over Your children. Amen."

Devotion 90

Scripture:

"Father, I have sinned against heaven and against you" (Luke 15:18).

All the children were yelling and shouting at the same time. Every one of them were saying mean things back and forth. Faces were getting red and tears were beginning when Dad walked in.

"What's going on here?" Dad demanded. The children were quiet for a second. Then he asked, "Who started this?" and they all began again, talking at once and pointing fingers and crying some more. Not one of them said, "I started it," or "It's all my fault."

It's really hard to admit you are wrong. It is really hard to say, "I have sinned." In this case, most all of the children were responsible for some of the fighting. Things got better when each one admitted their share of guilt and apologized.

It may be hard but it is good for us when we admit we are wrong and apologize. It is especially good for us when we admit we are wrong and confess our sins to God. When we are truly sorry and ask Jesus to forgive us, He will take away our guilt. He can do this, remember, because He took the punishment for all our wrongdoing when He died on the cross.

Let's Talk:

When was the last time you admitted you were wrong? Is it hard for you to say you are sorry? Talk about a time when there was a problem between you and another person and when you said you were sorry, it got better.

To Learn More:

For the complete story of a son who had to confess that he had sinned, read Luke 15:13–18.

Prayer:

"Dear Lord Jesus, please help us to say we are sorry when we need to. Forgive us for the sins that we have committed even this day. Thank You. For Your sake, amen."

Devotion 91

. . . .

Scripture:

Depart from evil, and do good (Psalm 34:14 KJV).

Four-year-old Larry saw some bees flying in and out of a hole in the side of a ditch. To see where they went, he poked a stick into the hole, trying to make it bigger. A lot more bees came out, buzzing really fast and loud. He poked the hole again, and the bees swarmed all around him with their angry buzzing. He started to swat at them and tried to get away, but by then they were all over him, all over his shirt, and stinging him like crazy. He began to scream as he ran toward the house. His mother came running to help. She yanked off his shirt, grabbed him in her arms, and hurried inside.

Larry cried as mom put him in a tub of warm water and sponged his many stings with soda. "I wish those bad bees went away from me," he said sadly. "Why did they get on me? Why did they sting me?"

With loving concern Mother explained to him, "Larry, if you don't want to get stung, you have to stay away from the bees."

Sometimes we wonder what made us sin. We think that we tried and tried not to. But where did we put ourselves? If you really really want something you see in the store but you don't have the money, standing there looking at it will just make you want it worse. Get away from it! If you put yourself with companions who misuse God's name, if you go to a party where everyone is drinking, if your friends are all having sex or doing drugs, can you just keep looking on and looking on and not do as they do? You need to get out, get away. If you are tempted to do any wrong thing, maybe it is time to get yourself away from the sin and put yourself in a better place.

Let's Talk:

Have you ever found yourself in a situation where you felt you had to do wrong and there was no choice? Would it have helped to have departed from the evil much sooner? Is there really such a thing as "I couldn't help it" when it comes to doing wrong?

To Learn More:

For further meditation, read all of Psalm 34.

. . . .

Prayer:

"Dear Father, help us to flee from evil and pursue that which is good. In Jesus' name we pray, amen."

Devotion 92

Scripture:

Turn from evil and do good (Psalm 34:14).

It's interesting to notice that in this verse God doesn't just tell us what not to do—evil, but He also tells us what to do—good.

Jodi wasn't that bad of a person. She was pretty nice to people, and she usually didn't cheat too much on tests or homework, maybe just a little. Fear of getting caught usually stopped her. She had only been drunk once and didn't think it was too cool to be so "out of it," so she toned it down a bit, even though she enjoyed the high school party scene. The idea that she shouldn't drink because she was younger than the drinking age never even entered her mind. She hadn't had sex with her boyfriend but had been considering it when they broke up.

One day, a schoolmate invited her to a Young Life meeting. There Jodi learned about God's love for her, Christ's sacrifice, and how to become a Christian. After awhile, she joined God's family. As time went on, she found herself more and more busy with Young Life activities. She even got involved in a church and it's youth group. She decided to sing in the youth choir and help out in the nursery. Over time, she found she was not going to drinking parties anymore, and gradually her friends had changed. With friends who loved God, her speech changed, and she no longer used His name carelessly. She learned about God's standards of truth and decided to be totally honest in her school work. After a week at Young Life camp, she made a commitment to stay sexually pure. She was so busy with Young Life and the youth group, which in turn made her busy helping others, that one day she realized she hadn't been to a drinking party for a long time. It was an exciting day for her when she went into the city with her youth group to feed street people.

This story is the ideal. But the point is, when a person becomes new in Christ, the old just doesn't go, the new does come (2 Corinthians 5:17). Jodi didn't just flee evil, she also began to do good. God doesn't just say, "don't, don't." He also says, "do, do." And both the dos and the don'ts are for our good, His glory, and the good of others.

Let's Talk:

Have you ever started to feel like being God's child was too negative, just a bunch of don'ts? Think about all the dos in God's Word and try them!

To Learn More:

For another thought on doing good, read Romans 12:21.

Prayer:

"Dear Lord, help us to be too busy doing good to do any wrong. Thank You. Amen."

Devotion 93

. . . .

Scripture:

Jesus Christ is the same yesterday and today and forever (Hebrews 13:8).

Susan was upset again and went to her mom with yet another problem with her friend Janey.

"Mom, I just don't understand Janey. Yesterday she wanted to hang around with me at school, and we were friends. Today she acted mean and kept giving me put-downs all the time."

"Did you try to tell her how you feel, like we talked about before?" asked Mother.

"Yes, and I thought she was going to be nice. But she wasn't."

"Well, you and I know that we both get grouchy sometimes, and we take it out on each other. Maybe she has bad days at home and takes them out on you. Maybe she's extra tired sometimes or even hungry if she doesn't eat a good lunch. Maybe she thought you were mean or angry to her! Any of those things can make a person grouchy, and when you're grouchy you often take it out on whoever is handy."

"Yeah, well, I just wish I had one friend who never changed, who I could count on always being the same with me," lamented Susan.

"You do," said Mother. "Jesus is a friend that 'stays closer than a brother,' and He is 'the same yesterday, today, and forever.'"

"Wow!" exclaimed Susan. "I know that sometimes Jesus calls Himself our friend, but I never thought about the fact that He never changes. I'm glad, Mom, and I'm glad I can talk to both you and God about my problems."

Let's Talk:

What are some times you can call on Jesus who is your best Friend?

To Learn More:

For further meditation, read Deuteronomy 31:5–6.

Prayer:

"Dear Lord, thank You that You are always there and always the same. In Jesus' name, amen."

. . . .

Devotion 94

Scripture:

There is neither Jew nor Greek, slave nor free, male nor female, for you are all one in Christ Jesus (Galatians 3:28).

The kids were upset. On a night near Halloween, several people had come to the football game dressed in Ku Klux Klan outfits.

"Don't people understand what the Klan represents? How could Christians identify themselves with racism or any group that advocates one group of people being superior to another?" questioned Tammy with obvious distress.

She was right. God's Word is very clear that God is the creator of all human beings. And the verse above tells us that when it comes to salvation, we are all one in Christ Jesus. All of us have sinned, and all of us for whom Christ died can be forgiven and be part of God's family. If we are all part of the same family, we cannot hold biased opinions against any group of people.

This experience led to a good discussion on racism in our home, and eventually, the school addressed the subject of prejudice in an assembly. The students were reminded that mocking or excluding someone for any exterior difference is not pleasing to God.

Let's Talk:

Have you ever got caught up in the kidding attitude of putting down another race or culture? Do you think it's an okay thing to do? If you live in a place where there aren't many people of different skin colors or varying backgrounds, what can you do as a family to become accepting of those differences?

To Learn More:

For further thought, read Galatians 3:26–4:7.

Prayer:

"Dear Father in heaven, please fill us with Your love, and help us to never prejudge others on the basis of skin color. We confess that we are all prejudiced in some way. Please help us to overcome our biases and realize we are all equal at the Cross. In Jesus' name, amen."

Devotion 95

Scripture:
For anyone who does not love his brother, whom he has seen, cannot love God, whom he has not seen (1 John 4:20).

One day Tammy and Becky went to the grocery store. In one aisle they saw a woman who reminded them so much of their birth mother it made Tammy's heart jump! Then of course they realized that she was their cousin, one they hadn't seen in awhile, and she was about the same age as their mom had been when she died.

In a family of blood relatives you will often see the same color eyes, the same shaped nose, the same build, a similar walk, or the same smile in many different individuals. If we are members of God's family, if God is our Father, we will have some of His characteristics.

John writes in his epistle that God is love, and if we are His children than we will love our brothers and sisters in Christ. This verse helps to strengthen the lesson from yesterday. John challenged the church he wrote to in his epistle, telling them that to think they were lovers of God while not acting in loving ways toward other members of God's family was wrong. He says if you truly know God, are truly a part of God's family, you will show that you are part of the family by having family characteristics, and in this case, you will have love. He says in a further verse (verse 21) that "Whoever loves God must love his brother."

Let's Talk:
If God our Father is love, what will be some characteristics of love that everyone in His family will have?

To Learn More:
To hear more about love, read 1 John 4:7–21.

Prayer:
"Dear Jesus, help us to love one another as You loved us and gave Yourself for us. In Your name and for Your glory we pray. Amen."

Devotion 96

Scripture:

'Do not seek revenge or bear a grudge against one of your people, but love your neighbor as yourself. I am the Lord' (Leviticus 19:18).

When Aaron and Andrew were little, they would often play with each other's toys. Sometimes Andrew would break Aaron's toy, or, in the case of construction toys, he would take apart or mess up Aaron's creations. Sometimes Aaron would break Andrew's toys or mess up his creations. The offended party would then get angry with his brother for doing these things and do something to pay him back. Sometimes they would hide each other's toys or break one on purpose. Other times, they would get into a knock-down-drag-out wrestling match and try to beat each other up, all to get even, to get revenge.

When the girls were younger and they would get mad at each other, they would hide each other's things, pout, or simply not speak to each other. This could last awhile. This is called "bearing a grudge."

Children who live together often do these kinds of things or at least feel like doing them. But this verse teaches us to forgive, not to try to get revenge and not to bear a grudge. Getting revenge and bearing a grudge is just like hating someone, and as we have talked about so many times before, God wants us to love, not to hate.

Let's Talk:

Do you sometimes feel that you are just SO angry that you can't forgive your brother or sister? Do you feel like getting revenge, or do you act like you have a grudge? (Answer silently, to yourself.) Remember that you can ask God to help you love. Also, Mom and Dad may be able to help set limits that are acceptable to both kids who are disagreeing, and if all of you stay within those limits, perhaps you will have less reason to get mad.

To Learn More:

For more on getting along, read Leviticus 19:1–4, 9–37.

Prayer:

"Dear Jesus, once again we ask You to help us love one another. For Your sake we pray. Amen."

Devotions for the Blended Family

Devotion 97

Scripture:
If a man will not work, he shall not eat (2 Thessalonians 3:10).

At our house, everyone has regular chores. Each person is responsible to keep his or her own room picked up and clean; each day someone helps clean up after meals, and there is a household chore for each child to do on "housework day." We are all supposed to pick up after ourselves (although none of us do this perfectly). We have these policies to keep order in our busy, crowded household. But we also do it because the Bible teaches us that it is the right thing to do.

When our children are grown up, they will need the self-discipline and skills of knowing how to work, even when they may sometimes not feel like it. People have to work in order to get money for food, clothing, and shelter, and God wants us to be good workers. Giving our children experience now will help them later.

There was a man at a certain company who spent a lot of his time walking around and talking to others. When his boss asked him what he was doing, he would say he was on his way to do this or that, but he really never did much. Finally, his boss fired him. The man was able to do his job; he just didn't want to. There are some people who are sick or disabled so they can't work, or some people who can't find a job for a time. We should be glad to help them out. But if anyone will not work, then, God says, he simply won't have the food he needs to eat.

Let's Talk:
Have you ever known someone who refused to work? What happened to that person? When you don't feel like taking care of your things or helping around the house, would it help you to remember what God's Word says?

To Learn More:
Read 2 Thessalonians 3:7–14 for the apostles' policy on work.

Prayer:
"Dear Jesus, please give us the strength and desire to work for all that we have. For Your glory we pray. Amen."

Devotion 98

Scripture:

For God did not give us a spirit of timidity, but a spirit of power, of love and of self-discipline (2 Timothy 1:7).

Give thanks to the LORD, for he is good. His love endures forever (Psalm 136:1).

Becky was grouchy. "I hate science; I just know I'm going to get a bad grade. I hate my teacher; I hate school," were some of her after-school remarks.

Later, she was combing her hair, and as soon as her mom walked by, she started to grumble, "I hate my hair, it never turns out right. I wish it was a different color. My legs are fat, etc. etc."

When Mom or Dad or one of the other kids tried to get her to cheer up, or if they gave her a compliment, she just found something else to criticize or complain about. Nobody could do anything to change her mood. But Becky could.

Becky learned that she had a problem with depression, and she could continue in it, or she could take control of her attitude and do something about it. She learned that for her, it was important to get exercise every day. Being outside and having a good work-out would not only help her to feel cheerful but also help her to sleep better. Better rest also helped her to be more cheerful. But one of the greatest things that she learned was to fill her mind with God's Word. She put verses from Psalm 136 and other verses about God's blessings and promises on note cards. When she began to feel down in the dumps, she could change her feelings by changing her way of thinking. When she thought more about God's power and His blessing in her life, she was able to think and feel much more positively about herself and her life.

Some depression is chemical and requires medical treatment. But the day-to-day blues that we all get at times can be turned around when we discipline our minds to think the way God wants us to think.

Let's Talk:

Have you ever felt "down" and had your feelings change

when you began to think differently? If you feel down, do you want to be left alone, or do you want your family to try to cheer you up? Each person is different, and it helps us to know what works for you.

To Learn More:

For further meditation on the unfailing love of God, read all of Psalm 136.

Prayer:

"Dear Father, we give ourselves, even our moods, to You. Help us not to hurt others when we are down. Thank You for Your Word which can comfort and restore us. Thank You that You never stop loving us, even when we're grouchy. In Your name and for Your glory we pray. Amen."

Devotion 99

Scripture:

"Be strong and courageous. Do not be afraid or terrified because of them, for the LORD your God goes with you; he will never leave you, nor forsake you" (Deuteronomy 31:6).

Though my father and mother forsake me, the LORD will receive me (Psalm 27:10).

Moses had been the leader of God's people for many many years. Now he was going to go away. It was time for him to die. But he did not leave his people without a leader and a guide. God chose Joshua to lead the people in Moses' place. But most importantly, in Deuteronomy 31, Moses tells the people not to be afraid, but to trust because God will always be with them.

If you are living in a blended family, a parent left either because there was a divorce or because of death. There may have been and may still be times when you hurt inside because you are lonely for the parent who is gone. Maybe you feel angry that he or she left, maybe you wonder if they really love you. Maybe you are afraid that the parent you have will go away, too. Sometimes kids with stepparents are afraid to love or accept them because they are afraid if they start to like them and depend on them, the stepparents may leave the way their first parents did. These verses contain very special promises for kids with these kinds of fears. God's Word is assuring us that no matter what our earthly parents may do, He will never forsake us. If we are children of God, He promises to be with us all the time. Anytime you need someone to talk to, God is there. Anytime you are lonely or afraid, you can ask Him to be with you and He is.

Let's Talk:

Have you been or are you afraid to love your stepparent because you fear he or she may leave? Maybe you could talk this over with the parents you are with. Have you ever felt alone and decided to pray? Did talking to God help? Share with each other times when you have felt comforted.

To Learn More:

For further meditation, read Isaiah 49:15–16.

Prayer:

"Dear Jesus, thank You that You are always with us. Amen."

Devotion 100

Scripture:

And we know that in all things God works for the good of those who love him, who have been called according to his purpose (Romans 8:28).

Yesterday we talked about the pain you may have felt and may still feel because one of your parents is gone. Now you may have a stepparent, and that may or may not be a comfort to you. But God promises that if we are His children, He is at work, making even the pain and the sorrow into a good thing. The question to ask yourself is: do I have a willing heart, freely saying, "God do what You want in my life"? If we stay angry all the time, we will never learn what God wants to teach us through our pain. If we try to ignore the sad feelings and push them down, they will keep us from receiving comfort. You may tell God, tell a parent, or tell a counselor how you feel. But remember, in all things and at all times God *is* working for good. He can even take the bad stuff and turn it around for good.

Let's Talk:

Are you letting yourself trust in His plan?

To Learn More:

For further meditation, read Romans 8:28–38.

Prayer:

"Dear Jesus, please help me to believe that You are at work for good. Help me to trust You more with all of my life, even when bad things happen. In Your name, and for Your glory I pray. Amen."

Devotion 101

∙ ∙

Scripture:

"But I tell you that anyone who is angry with his brother will be subject to judgment. Again, anyone who says to his brother, 'Raca,' is answerable to the Sanhedrin. But anyone who says, 'You fool!' will be in danger of the fire of hell" (Matthew 5:22).

Back in Jesus' time when people were angry at other people, they would call them names, just like people today sometimes do. They would say *raca* or "fool." You may say "dummy," "butthead," "jerk," or even worse. You know what kind of words you use. The Sanhedrin were the rulers or judges of Jesus' time. They would decide if someone had harmed someone else with words and maybe fine that person or put him or her in jail. Jesus says don't let your anger get so out of control that you are in danger of judgment.

You may feel angry sometimes with one parent or another. You may feel especially angry with the brothers or sisters with whom you must share living space. But Jesus wants us to make sure that we don't let our anger get out of control. He doesn't want us to be calling names or doing things to destroy another person's feelings. Talk about what makes you feel angry. Decide together with your parents and siblings what are good limits to each person's property and space. Be forgiving. We all mess up and violate someone's space sometimes.

Let's Talk:

What makes you the most angry? Can you talk about it? If you can't solve the problem with your parents, maybe this is one of those things that you will need outside help for. Remember, too, that you can ask God for wisdom in how to get along (James 1), and He will give it. But make up your mind that no matter how angry you are, you won't call names.

To Learn More:

For further meditation, read Matthew 5:21–25.

Prayer:

"Dear Jesus, help us to obey You and not call each other names. In Your name, amen."

∙ ∙

Devotion 102

Scripture:

"I have loved you with an everlasting love; I have drawn you with loving-kindness" (Jeremiah 31:3).

Jason walked into the house with his head hung low, his arms dangling. He was feeling very low and lonely. His father was due to visit today; Jason expected him to pick him up at school. But he never came. Because it was late, Jason missed the bus and had to walk home. His mom was at work and he had no one to talk to. Finally, his older sister came home. She sat down at the piano and started to practice.

"Hi, Janey," called Jason. "Aren't you mad that dad didn't come for us like he promised?"

"Oh Jason, I hardly believe him anymore. You know he left us just after you were born. And he misses his times with us so often, I just try to never count on him until I see him," his sister replied. "It hurts less if you don't expect him to keep his promises."

"Yeah, well, I guess I was really hoping," sighed Jason. "Our stepdad is nice I guess. But I'm curious about our real dad. I want to know him. Doesn't he even love us?"

"I don't know if he loves us," said Janey. "But I know that Mom loves us. And Grandma and Grandpa, they love us all the time and no matter what. And I think our stepdad kind of likes us a lot too. But the best thing is Jason, God loves us. Remember that verse we read at the table last night? 'God loves us with everlasting love and draws us with lovingkindness.'"

Jason gave a little laugh. "Oh yeah, Mom said that 'drawing us with lovingkindness' doesn't mean that God draws pictures of us but that He hugs us to Himself. That's cool."

Let's Talk:

Have you ever felt like Jason? Have you ever wondered if your parent who left even cares for you? Talk about it with your family. Remember—God's love is everlasting!

To Learn More:

For further meditation, read Romans 8:35–39.

Prayer:

"Dear Lord Jesus, thank You that You love us and never leave us. Help us to feel that You are near. In Your name, amen."

Devotion 103

Scripture:

How great is the love the Father has lavished on us, that we should be called children of God! (1 John 3:1).

There is more to yesterday's story. That night Jason and Janey's mother and stepfather, whose name is Bill, wanted to talk something over with the kids. Bill ask them if they would like him to adopt them. They would legally be his children, his and their mom's complete responsibility. They would have new last names, the same name their mom got when she married him. Would they want to do this? They could visit their own dad if their mom and Bill thought it was okay, but the law would not say they had to, like it did now. It would be a big step.

Janey and Jason did not make up their minds right away. They had grown pretty fond of Bill in the year he and their mom had been married. They liked him most of the time, but they weren't sure that they loved him, not yet anyway. They weren't sure they could trust him not to leave them. But they thought, *Wow! A dad who wants us be his responsibility, a dad who wants to share in our care and wants to give us his name!* The fact that Bill wanted them to be his children made them feel special.

When we are born, we are *natural* children, children of the flesh. If we accept what Jesus did for us when He died on the cross for our sins, if we *repent*, turning from our own selfish way of living to living a life for God, then we become *born again*, or adopted into God's family. God adopts us the way a stepparent might, and gives us His name, the name of *Christian*, or "child of God."

Let's Talk:

Answer these questions silently, to yourself. Have you been adopted by Jesus? Have you given yourself to Him, to be called a child of God?

To Learn More:

To learn more about what it's like to be a child of God, read 1 John 3:1–6.

Prayer:

"Dear Lord Jesus, thank You that You died for me. Please forgive my sins, and take over my life. For Your glory, amen."

Devotion 104

Scripture:

In love he predestined us to be adopted as his sons, through Jesus Christ, in accordance with his pleasure and will (Ephesians 1:5).

Yesterday we talked about getting adopted and having a new name. This verse tells us that God planned for (predestined) us who believe to become His children. And not only was our spiritual adoption His will, but it was His pleasure! He wants us to be His children, to have His name, and our becoming children of God brings Him pleasure!

It is so very special to be adopted by parents who love you and choose you to be their child. But it is even more special that God Himself takes pleasure, is delighted, to make us His children. Over the next few days, we will talk about some of the privileges of being adopted children of God.

If you are a child of God, you have His name. That is, you are known as a Christian, a child of God.

Let's Talk:

Do you like being called a Christian? Are you proud to be known as a child of God?

To Learn More:

Read Romans 8:31–38 for some promises God makes to His adopted children.

Prayer:

"Dear Lord Jesus, we are not worthy to be called Your children, but You chose us, You adopted us. Please help us to love You faithfully. Amen."

Devotion 105

Scripture:

For I am convinced that neither death nor life, neither angels nor demons, neither the present nor the future, nor any powers, neither height or depth, nor anything else in all creation, will be able to separate us from the love of God that is in Christ Jesus our Lord (Romans 8:38–39).

Janey and Jason weren't sure yet if they could trust their stepfather enough to love him. The fact that he wanted to adopt them and to take responsibility for them helped their trust to grow.

But even if they never become totally sure that Bill will be a permanent father, they can be sure of God. The verse above tells us that NOTHING, absolutely nothing, can separate God's children from His love. Bill was willing to give the children his name and was willing to support them and to include them in his life plan. Jesus, the Son of God, was willing to give up all the wonders of heaven to come to earth and live as a man, and finally to give up His life as He died on the cross to take the punishment for our sins. He did this so that He could call all who believe "the children of God." If you believe that Jesus died for you, if you have turned from living a self-centered life to living a life centered on God, then you will never ever be separated from His love. Nothing that happened in the past, or that may happen in the future no matter where you go on this earth, whether to the highest mountain or the lowest valley, nor any powers of good or evil in your life, nothing, absolutely nothing, can separate you from the love of God!

Let's Talk:

Can you think of anything that would separate you from God's love?

To Learn More:

For more on this promise, read Romans 8:28–39.

Prayer:

"Dear Father God, thank You so much for Your promise never to leave us. Thank You that You are more powerful than anything that may happen in our lives. Help us to live as those who are called 'children of God.' Amen."

Devotion 106

Scripture:

For you did not receive a spirit that makes you a slave again to fear, but you received the Spirit of sonship. And by him we cry, "Abba, Father" (Romans 8:15).

When Bill told Jason and Janey that he wanted to adopt them, he was making a promise that he would not leave them and that they could come to him for help and guidance whenever they needed a father's hand with their lives. They wouldn't have to be afraid that he would ever say, "Go away, you're not my children." He wanted to make them his children, and they could even call him "Dad" or "Daddy" if they wanted to.

If we are God's children, there are some things that we don't have to be afraid of. We don't have to be afraid of God's judgment. As God's children, we know that Jesus took all the punishment that may be due to us for our wrongdoings. Even if we sin now and may suffer the natural consequences of those sins (see Devotion 82), we don't have to suffer eternal punishment. Another thing we never have to be afraid of is being separated from God. We never ever will. We talked about this yesterday.

Not only are we never separated from God's love, we can come to Him whenever we need to (Hebrews 4:16), for comfort and wisdom (James 1), and we can call out to Him in a familiar and affectionate way. The *Abba, Father* in the verse is like saying "Dad" or "Daddy."

Let's Talk:

What pictures come into your mind when you think of God as "Daddy"? How does it make you feel to know that nothing can separate you from God's love?

To Learn More:

For more about being free from fear of judgment and free to live as children of God, read all of Romans 8:1–17.

Prayer:

"Dear Lord, thank You that You are our heavenly "dad," always available and always there for us. Thank You that You will never leave us. In Jesus' name, amen."

Devotion 107

Scripture:

Now if we are children, then we are heirs—heirs of God and co-heirs with Christ . . . (Romans 8:17).

If Janey and Jason decide to let Bill adopt them, they will become his children in every legal way. They will be his "heirs." To be an *heir* means that they are entitled to all that is his if he should die. And while he lives, it means that they are under his protection and care, that he will provide for all their needs.

Jesus Christ is the only "natural" Son of God. But any of us who have been "adopted" by God's gracious forgiveness of our sins is a co-heir with Christ. This is sort of like being a stepbrother or stepsister to Jesus. But we are not just the stepchildren by marriage, we are children that have been fully adopted and entitled to the inheritance, a part of the family of God in every legal way. That means that we wear the name of Christ—we are called "Christian," that God our Father will never leave us or forsake us and that one day we will be taken to heaven to live and reign with Him. What a glorious inheritance we have in Christ Jesus!

Let's Talk:

What are some more privileges of heirs of your family on earth? of the family of God?

To Learn More:

For more about being God's chosen, adopted children, read John 1:12–13.

Prayer:

"Dear Father in heaven, thank You for making us Your children. Help us to live, as Your heirs, lives that reflect Your likeness in us. In Jesus' name, amen."

Devotion 108

Scripture:

How great is the love the Father has lavished on us, that we should be called children of God! And that is what we are! (1 John 3:1).

It is so wonderful to be adopted by a parent or parents that choose you and love you. But it is even more wonderful to know that God has loved and chosen us to be His own dear children. This verse says that He has "lavished" us with His love. *Lavished* is a wonderful word. It means that His love is extravagantly generous and liberal in its expression. He loves us so extravagantly that He calls us and makes us His own dear children! It is a great and awesome thing to think that we are called God's children, but it's even greater and more awesome to realize that we really are His children. Very old manuscripts of this verse in the Bible say, "and we are so— really His children." To be loved and adopted not by anything that we have done but because of His grace, His love and forgiveness toward us, what a wondrous thing!

Sometimes, kids who for one reason or another aren't sure of their parents love aren't sure of God's love either. If one parent has left and you worry about losing the other one, if a parent is getting remarried and you are afraid it means he or she won't be your parent anymore (he or she will), any of these things may make it difficult for you to feel how much God loves you. So I picked this verse to read again and to remind you that not only does God love you, He lavishes His love on you so much that He actually calls you His child—because you are!

Let's Talk:

Do you ever have a hard time believing God loves you? Do you ever have a hard time believing your parents love you? Remember, God's love is unfailing and perfect.

To Learn More:

For more on being God's child, read Romans 8:15–17.

Prayer:

"Dear Lord, thank You for making me Your child. Help me to believe in Your love and to feel it as You lavish it upon me. In Jesus' name, amen."

Devotion 109

Scripture:

The gray-haired and the aged are on our side . . . (Job 15:10).

Daniel's parents were divorced when he was very young. He only saw his father a few times, and he had only seen his paternal grandparents once in his whole life. When Daniel grew up and became engaged to be married, he admitted to his fiancé that he had a longing inside to get to know his father's side of his family better. So they invited them to the wedding. Even though it was a long way to come, his father came, and his grandpa wrote a nice letter and sent a gift! Daniel was so happy! Each year he and his wife exchange a few letters and make a few phone calls to his grandparents. When they had a baby they made sure they sent pictures to "Grandpa Gerth." Getting to know his grandparents made Daniel feel more complete, made him feel like he knew and understood himself better, made him feel like he knew where he belonged in the scheme of life.

Because children of divorce don't live with both their parents, they may not get to see one set or the other of their natural grandparents very often. But grandparents are important. Contact with grandparents is valuable to children's identity and development, helping them to know, like Daniel, more about themselves and where they fit in. During difficult times of adjustment when children are getting used to a different way of living, continued relationships with grandparents can make a big difference in how secure they feel.

Let's Talk:

Do you miss seeing your grandparents? Is it possible to work out a way to see them more?

To Learn More:

For more about grandparents, you may want to read Proverbs 17:6 and 2 Timothy 1:3–5.

Prayer:

"Dear Father in heaven, help us to find a way to include our grandparents in our lives. Thank You for them. In Jesus' name, amen."

Devotion 110

Scripture:

I will sing of the LORD's great love forever; with my mouth I will make your faithfulness known through all generations (Psalm 89:1).

When we married, we promised that we would make a real effort to keep in touch with grandparents on all sides. This means that despite the fact that a parent is deceased, our children still know their grandparents and others on that side of the family. This has been a great help as they form their identities. They can say, "I like sports the way the Smith family does." Or, "I love literature and classical music the way my dad's father does." "I'm a lot like Grandpa or Grandma So and So, aren't I?" And remember the story about Tammy seeing a woman in the store who was so much like her mom? That would have been really creepy if she didn't know who her relatives were!

It has not always been easy keeping in touch with the multiple sets of grandparents and great-grandparents. Probably not one of them feels like they have adequate attention from us. But we try. From being around the oldest great-grandparents, our children have also learned something about maintaining a loving and caring attitude toward the aged and dying. But the greatest heritage of all has been to know their grandparents' faith and to see how God has been faithful in their lives. Being offspring of those who love God to the third and the fourth generation has made them strong in their faith and given them a perception of where they fit into God's family and God's plan for the world. Our lives are enriched by our children's grandparents!

Let's Talk:

If you don't ever see your grandparents on the side of your deceased or non-custodial parent, could you? Can you see that it would be good for your family? Maybe it wouldn't be good in every case. But do think about it and talk about how seeing them would make you feel.

To Learn More:

For more about God's faithfulness to generations, read Psalm 89:1–4.

Prayer:

"Dear Father God, thank You that You have been faithful throughout all generations of those that love You. Thank You for our grandparents. In Jesus' name, amen."

Devotion 111

Scripture:

And surely I am with you always . . . (Matthew 28:20).

Robbie and Kalee were on a visit to their mom and stepfather's house. They had been living with their dad ever since their mom left when they were little. In the home where they lived, their dad and stepmother always had devotions with them at the table and tucked them into bed at night. At their house, no one swore. Now they were at their mom's. Here they didn't pray at meals or have devotions at the table. Their mom was nice enough to them, but she and her husband had a coarse way of talking and thought nothing of using the Lord's name carelessly. It made them feel uneasy. One minute they would think they didn't like their mother for being like this, the next minute they would feel guilty because they knew they should love her because she was their mother.

"Robbie, I miss Dad," lamented Kalee when they were alone. "At our house I feel safer. I want to go home."

"Sometimes I want to go home, too" replied Robbie. "It IS different here. But do you remember what Dad read in our devotions the last night we were at home?"

"Something about God being with us?" Kalee tried to recall.

"Yes. Dad read that verse where Jesus told His disciples He was with them always," answered Robbie.

Remembering that they were God's children and that God was with them always and everywhere made Kalee and Robbie feel more secure when they were away from home.

Let's Talk:

Do you feel uneasy when you visit your other parent's house and things are not the same? Remember that you can talk to God about your worries. Maybe you can talk to the parent you visit and tell him or her what makes you feel uncomfortable or afraid. That may reassure you. But whether Mom or Dad can comfort you or not, remember that Jesus promised to be with you always.

To Learn More:

You may want to read Isaiah 41:10 and Deuteronomy 31:6 for more reassurance of God's continual presence.

Prayer:

"Dear Father God, thank You that You never leave us. Help us to feel Your presence. In Jesus' name, amen."

Devotion 112

Scripture:

My command is this: Love each other as I have loved you (John 15:12).

But God demonstrates his own love for us in this: While we were still sinners, Christ died for us (Romans 5:8).

Sometimes, when those who are called "the children of God" have been living the life of a Christian for a long time, when they have come to love God's Word and God's law and have begun to live daily for God, sometimes they become impatient and intolerant of those who have not. From these verses we are reminded that God showed His love for us by sending Jesus to die for our sins BEFORE we repented, and that we are commanded to love one another the way He loves us. How does He love us? He lay down His life for us (John 15:13) while we were still sinners (Romans 5:8).

Sometimes, if one parent's home is a Christian home and one parent's home is not, you may feel confused. You may feel like looking down on the parent or stepsiblings who are not Christians. Or, you may like the non-Christian home better. If we obey Jesus, we will try to love one another in all different circumstances. It is tough going back and forth from one home to another with different rules and different ways of doing things. But we can learn, with God's help, to be tolerant and patient. It is especially important, as we have said before, to talk with your parents about how you are feeling. Tell them what causes you the most distress or difficulty. See if some things can change. And when they can't change, pray for God's strength to help you. Do you remember Philippians 4:13? "I can do everything through him who gives me strength."

Let's Talk:

What is the hardest thing for you when going from one parent's house to the other? Let's pray about it together.

To Learn More:

For more about God's love and loving one another, read John 15: 9–17.

Prayer:

"Dear Jesus, please help the children as they go from one home to the other. Help them to be loving to all their parents. May they know that their parents keep loving them whether they are with them or not. Help them to know that You will give them strength and You will never leave them. Thank You. Amen."

Devotion 113

Scripture:

The day is thine, the night is also thine (Psalm 74:16 KJV).

Never will I leave you (Hebrews 13:5).

Three-year-old Margaret did not want to go into her bedroom in the new house. "I don't want to, it's dark in there," worried Margaret.

"Go in, turn on the light, get into bed, and I'll be there in a minute," said mother as she fed the baby.

"I'm afraid, it's dark," Margaret insisted.

"Don't be afraid, dear, Jesus is there, even in the dark," assured her mother.

"Well, if Jesus is in there, then why doesn't He turn on the light?!"

This is one of those family stories that my parents tell my children about me. It is true that God is with us everywhere and that the night is His, just like the day. Sometimes, when we are in different places, especially at night, we may feel afraid. But when we feel afraid, we can remember that God made the night and that He is with us wherever we go. He promises never to leave us or forsake us.

Let's Talk:

Have you ever been afraid of the dark or afraid of staying in a new place? If you are afraid, would it help to remind yourself to trust that Jesus is there?

To Learn More:

For more assurance that God is with you, read Hebrews 13:5–6.

Prayer:

"Dear Jesus, help us not to be afraid. Help us to believe that You are with us and that You will never leave us. Thank You for Your presence. In Your name we pray. Amen."

Devotion 114

. . . .

Scripture:
For God so loved the world that he gave his one and only Son, that whoever believes in him shall not perish but have eternal life (John 3:16).

He [God] is patient with you, not wanting anyone to perish, but everyone to come to repentance (2 Peter 3:9).

When we read John 3:16, we can see that God offers the gift of "salvation" to anyone who believes. *Salvation* means deliverance from evil, from sin. God forgives us for our sins when we come to Him asking forgiveness and being willing to repent. (Remember, *repent* means to turn from living a life centered on self and selfish desires to one centered on God and what God desires for you.) The verses above remind us how patient God is, giving everyone a chance to be free from their sin by coming to repentance. I chose these verses to remind us of God's attitude toward those who have not received Him. Someday, judgment will come (Matthew 25:31–46). But until then He patiently waits for all who will to come. We cannot do less. If God is patient and loving, we also need to be patient and loving with those who have not come to repentance.

God does not, and we do not, have to love the evil deeds or bad behavior of others. But we must "love one another as I have loved you" and He loved us "while we were still sinners."

Let's Talk:
What are some specific actions we can do that are patient and loving to people who haven't yet repented of their sins and received God's gift?

To Learn More:
For more about God's love, His gift to us, and how we should respond to His gift, read John 3:16–21.

Prayer:
"Dear Lord, help us to be patient and loving with those who do not love You. Thank You for dying for our sins. In Jesus' name, amen."

. . . .

Devotion 115

Scripture:

"Enter through the narrow gate. For wide is the gate and broad is the road that leads to destruction, and many enter through it. But small is the gate and narrow the road that leads to life, and only a few find it" (Matthew 7:13–14).

Dad was reading devotions on a day close to Easter. The family began to discuss all that Jesus gave up for us. Then Mom asked, "What have we ever given up for God?"

She was surprised to hear what the kids had to say. One child mentioned how every time he puts some of his money in the offering plate, he is conscious of making a sacrifice for God. He doesn't earn much, so giving away some of it seems like quite a sacrifice! One of the children mentioned the movies they couldn't watch or the music we discourage listening to because the messages are too violent or negative. Then one of the older kids said, "We give up pre-marital sex for God. That's a pretty big thing!"

And so Mom and Dad realized that the gate their children had entered and the road they walk is narrow indeed. Not many of their peers choose to walk it, which makes our children sometimes feel alone as they try to live for God. They know many of the kids in their high school are having premarital sex and seem to get away with it. (That is, they haven't gotten a disease or pregnant.) They hear about the parties where "everyone" drinks. They talk about others who listen to every kind of music and see any movie.

We should not be surprised at all the people who do not care about living for God or obeying His Word. Jesus said there are few that enter at the narrow gate, and few walk the straight and narrow way. If we keep this in mind, it may help us to be further patient and accepting of those who live differently. Remember, we can be accepting and kind to the person, while not accepting or approving of his or her deeds.

Let's Talk:

What have you ever given up for God?

To Learn More:

For encouragement in the Christian life, read Hebrews 10:22–24.

Prayer:

"Dear Father, help us to be faithful and obedient, even when those around us are not. In Jesus' name, amen."

Devotion 116

Scripture:

How can a young [person] keep [his or her way] pure? By living according to your word. . . . . I have hidden your word in my heart that I might not sin against you (Psalm 119:9, 11).

Yesterday we said that not many people walk on the straight and narrow way, the way of God. With so many people around us doing things that are contrary to God's Word, it may become difficult at times for us to have obedient hearts. Perhaps schoolmates pressure you to do what they do. And what others do may look like fun, fun that we're missing! But these verses tell us how to keep ourselves pure. By following God's Word as a road map for our lives, by going so far as to hide His Word in our hearts we can keep our way pure. To *hide God's word in our hearts* means to read the Bible often and to memorize certain Scriptures. There are verses for almost every occasion, verses that, when called to mind, keep us from sinning against God. Here are some of those verses: 1 Corinthians 10:13, 1 John 4:4, Romans 8:37, and James 4:7.

Let's Talk:

Have you ever been tempted to do wrong and found that remembering something from God's Word made you strong enough to resist?

To Learn More:

To understand more about how God's Word keeps us from sin, you may like to read through Psalm 119.

Prayer:

"Dear Jesus, may we keep Your Word in our hearts, and may it truly keep us from sin. In Your name we pray. Amen."

Devotion 117

Scripture:

The heavens declare the glory of God; the skies proclaim the work of his hands (Psalm 19:1).

From Psalm 19 we learn that all "the heavens declare the glory of God." *Declare* is a way of speaking. This verse tells us that the silent heavens speak out the glory, the grandeur, the greatness, the awesomeness of God to all who are on the earth. The glory of the skies testifies to the righteousness and faithfulness of the Lord who created them.

One day after Aaron's nearly fatal bike accident, when he was still in the hospital, I decided to take a day off from going to see him and spend some time with my other children. We thought it would be fun to find a picnic spot in the woods behind our house. But as we walked across the back yard, we realized that the soft grass and shady tree area right on our own property was the best place to be. We enjoyed the sunshine and shade while eating, and then we laid on the grass and looked up at the summer sky. We talked about how wide and beautiful it was. We found pictures in the clouds and talked about God's creation and how He was taking care of us and watching over us at this difficult time. Taking time out to enjoy God's creation helped us feel assured of His watchful presence in our lives.

Let's Talk:

Have you ever looked at the sky, especially at night, and felt the awesomeness of God? If you live in town and can't see many stars, it can be fun to take your family out into the country at night, away from the lights of the city, and see how vast the starry sky really is. Looking at the sky can give a sense of God's greatness and of our part in His universe.

To Learn More:

For further meditation, read Psalm 19:1–6.

Prayer:

"Dear Lord, help us to see Your hand in all creation. Thanks for making the sky and for making us. In Jesus' name and for Your glory we pray. Amen."

Devotion 118

Scripture:

God blessed them and said to them, ". . . fill the earth and subdue it. Rule over the fish of the sea and the birds of the air and over every living creature that moves on the ground" (Genesis 1:28).

From the first book of the Bible, the book of Genesis, we learn that God created the earth and all that is within it. From this verse we learn that God wants human beings to rule the earth well.

Does keeping in mind the fact that we were created by God, just like the animals and the earth, make a difference in our attitude towards other forms of life? Knowing that both I and all of creation have our origins in God makes me have respect for all creation. Does it make you feel that way?

Let's Talk:

Do you think that because human beings are the highest form of intelligent life that they should have a right to abuse or neglect animals, such as pets and farm animals?

To Learn More:

Read Genesis 2:15 and Psalm 8:3–8 to learn more about the God-given relationship of human beings to the rest of creation.

Prayer:

"Dear heavenly Father, please help us to understand our part in Your creation. Help us to cherish all the works of Your hands. In Jesus' name and for Your glory we pray. Amen."

Devotion 119

Scripture:
God saw all that he had made, and it was very good (Genesis 1:31).

"Are not five sparrows sold for two pennies? Yet not one of them is forgotten by God" (Luke 12:6–7).

If we think about how God viewed His own creation, it may help us to get an idea about how to care for it. In Genesis 1:31 the Bible tells us that He looked at what He had made: human beings, animals, plants, and all the earth, and called them good. We are part of the creation of God just like all the other forms of life. If God values us and values those other living things, even a creature as small as a sparrow, then we should have respect for those other living things. If we are God's children, one of the traits of belonging to God's family should be that we value creation as our heavenly Father does.

Let's Talk:
If we as a part of God's family value creation, what does that mean in regard to the way we treat animals? If we value creation the way God does, what does that mean about our attitude toward polluting the countryside with rubbish, the waterways with waste, and the sky with poisonous emissions?

To Learn More:
To read a reminder that God gave the care of the earth to humankind, read Genesis 1:26–28, Genesis 2:15 and Psalm 8:3–8.

Prayer:
"Dear Father Creator, help us to care for this earth on which You have placed us. Make us wise in how we use the provisions of the world. May we take good care of all Your creation. In Jesus' name, amen."

Devotion 120

Scripture:

Wounds from a friend can be trusted, but an enemy multiplies kisses (Proverbs 27:6).

"Mom, oh—Mom," sobbed Karen as she came in the back door.

"What is it?" asked Mother with concern.

"A terrible thing happened today," explained Karen. "Elsie said my jeans were ripped in the back, and I should go to the office to get them fixed. I was embarrassed. I didn't want to believe her. I didn't want to think that I had been going around all morning with ripped jeans. Besides, I couldn't feel anything. Then Jennifer, a girl in the fifth grade said, 'Don't listen to Elsie. She's just trying to fool you. Your jeans are fine.' Mom, I believed her, and I didn't believe my friend," wailed Karen.

"All right, all right," comforted mother. "What happened next?"

"On the last recess when I went out to play, I saw Jennifer and a bunch of boys laughing and snickering at me. Then I realized she had lied on purpose just to embarrass me! I was embarrassed by what Elsie said, but at least it was the truth, and I could have done something about it! As it was, I was embarrassed so much worse, I was humiliated! And I went around all day with ripped pants! Why didn't I listen to Elsie?"

Sometimes our friends have to tell us something we don't like to hear. Sometimes our parents or brother or sister, someone who cares about us, tries to tell us we are doing something wrong or we have a problem. We don't want to hear it, so we don't listen. If someone cares about us and they have to tell us something unpleasant, it's usually for our own good. When we don't listen, when we don't accept "the wounds from a friend," we may end up getting wounded much worse.

Let's Talk:

Has something like that ever happened to you? Have you found out your friend was faithful, even when you didn't like what he or she had to say?

To Learn More:

For further meditation, read Proverbs 4:1–10.

Prayer:

"Dear Jesus, help us to be able to accept the truth about ourselves. Thank You for the strength You give us to change. In Your name, amen."

Devotion 121

Scripture:

Humble yourselves before the Lord, and he will lift you up (James 4:10).

Come near to God and he will come near to you (James 4:8).

"Get out of this room! This is my house! You just live here because your dad married my mom! Do you hear me?!? You have NO rights! This is MY house."

These awful words were shouted at Jodi by her stepsister Rhonda, with whom she had to share a room. They had been friends before their parents got married, but after they moved in together it had been nothing but war. Jodi desperately wanted to feel at home but instead felt shut out. Rhonda felt as if her home had been invaded. Jodi felt she had left the home she shared with her dad and given up her own room only to be treated like an outsider and never to feel "at home" again. Their parents couldn't afford to buy a bigger house. Before this incident both girls did their share of fighting for their rights. But now Jodi felt totally defeated. All she wanted was her own space, and she knew she would never get it. She was without hope.

God promises to lift up the humble and to comfort His children who draw near to Him. Jodi did that. She ran to the bathroom and cried and cried out to God. She felt His presence. She felt His love. When her dad and stepmother got home, she tried to tell them how she felt. She wasn't sure they understood. But they did began to talk about fixing a room for her in the basement.

When Rhonda heard what they were discussing, she asked, "Don't I get a new room too?"

"Why no, dear," said her mother. "You were so sure you wanted this room to yourself, you will have it. It will be yours completely. As soon as we're finished in the basement, you will never have to share your room with Jodi again."

Rhonda was jealous that the stepsister she hated would get the new room. But down deep inside she knew it was fair. Later, both of the girls were helped tremendously by having a few visits with the school social worker. They never got close, but they did learn to get along.

Let's Talk:

Is something like this going on at your house? Can you talk about it with your parents without getting out of control? If not, perhaps this is one of those times help from the outside is needed. Best of all, God promises that if we come near to Him, He will be near to us.

To Learn More:

For further meditation, read James 4:1–10.

Prayer:

"Dear Jesus, thank You for being near. Amen."

Devotion 122

Scripture:

But the fruit of the Spirit is love, joy, peace, patience, kindness, goodness, faithfulness, gentleness and self-control (Galatians 5:22–23).

Sisters are not the only ones who may feel invaded when a new stepparent and stepsiblings come to live. A mom or dad may feel invaded by the stepchildren that are brought into the home. I had boys; my husband had girls. Now I suddenly had girls, too, and he suddenly had boys. Now I couldn't get ready for church without sharing a bathroom. Many things were out of place in "my" bathroom, and often I couldn't find my comb or toiletries. Now Rog would go to get a tool, and it wouldn't be where he left it. Sometimes it would get left out in the weather. Patience can wear thin real fast when there are suddenly a lot more people living in a house at one time, using the same space and the same items. The children had to learn new limits. "This comb is just for Mom. Here is one for you to use just like it." "The kids can use all the tools in this toolbox, but they must not use the other ones." Everyone had to begin to think about other people's rights. Love and patience and kindness were the fruit of the Spirit we had to have grow in our daily lives very fast.

Let's Talk:

Talk about some of the "rights" that you feel were invaded when all of you moved in together. Have you set some limits? Is everyone comfortable with them? What are some reasonable limitations that you may set to allow for more peace among you?

To Learn More:

For further meditation, read Galatians 5:22–26.

Prayer:

"Dear Heavenly Father, please fill us with Your Spirit, and help us to have the fruit of that Spirit in our lives. Teach us how to live together. In Your name we pray. Amen."

Devotion 123

Scripture:

If the LORD delights in a man's way, he makes his steps firm; though he stumble, he will not fall, for the LORD upholds him with his hand (Psalm 37:23–24).

Sometimes we don't know exactly what to do in our lives. Sometimes we are faced with decisions to make and we don't know which choice is best. But if the Lord delights in our "way," that means, if we live the kind of life that pleases God, then He will help us walk the road of our lives. The promises of God to be with us and never leave us are true. But that doesn't mean that we won't have difficulties. This verse says that even when we stumble, we will not fall down, because the Lord will uphold us with His hand.

Let's Talk:

Can you think of a time you've stumbled, but God kept you from falling down?

To Learn More:

For further meditation, read Psalm 37:23–29.

Prayer:

"Dear Father God, thank You that You never leave us. Thank You that You are walking the road of life with us. Thank You that You hold us up and help us to not fall down. In Jesus' name, amen."

Devotion 124

Scripture:

But just as he who called you is holy, so be holy in all you do; for it is written: "Be holy, because I am holy" (1 Peter 1:15–16).

As children grow up there are many major life decisions to make: what kind of education to get, what kind of job to have, where to live, and whom to marry. Sometimes we feel very clearly what God's will is in these things, and other times we just don't know. But this verse reminds us that it's not the where and the what and the who of the decisions we make as much as it is *what we are.* Are we holy? Will that job or that place to live or marrying that person contribute to my holiness? Or, will that job or that person become a hinderance to my living a life of obedience? When we are in a tough spot, it is up to us to depend on the power of God for strength to overcome evil (remember putting on the full amour of God?). But when a decision first has to be made, asking whether this situation will strengthen my Christian walk or hinder it is a good question to ask.

Let's Talk:

Have you ever not known what to do, or what decision to make? Have you prayed and found wisdom? Have you ever had to just go ahead and make a decision without knowing for sure what was right? Remember, the important thing is to be an obedient child of God no matter where we are or what position we are in.

To Learn More:

For further meditation, read 1 Peter 1:13–21.

Prayer:

"Dear Jesus, make me more like You every day, in every way. Thank You for Your empowering Spirit. In Your name, amen."

Devotion 125

Scripture:

'These are my appointed feasts, the appointed feasts of the LORD, which you are to proclaim as scared assemblies' (Leviticus 23:2).

One man considers one day more sacred than another; another man considers every day alike. . . . He who regards one day as special, does so to the Lord (Romans 14:5–6).

The Lord *appointed*, that is, He designated, certain days as special for His people. Of course there was the Sabbath. From the time of creation God had set this day apart to rest and reflect (Genesis 2:2). But when He gave Moses the law, He gave him a list of other days, of "feast days" or holidays for them to celebrate. There are several reasons why God singled out some days to be more special than others. The special days of the Old Testament are probably not the same special days we celebrate now. But they still do the same thing—they help us remember what God has done for us. They are also days on which we can celebrate our family and celebrate the importance and achievements of the individual. In the next few devotional times we will be looking at the importance of family traditions, especially for a blended family.

Let's Talk:

Do you have trouble with holidays in your blended family? Can you think of reasons why celebrations and special days are important even if they may be difficult to get through? Would you like to celebrate more special days in your family? Talk about this and see if some of the things we discuss over the next few days will help.

To Learn More:

To read about a party in which Jesus was involved, read John 2:1–11.

Prayer:

"Dear Heavenly Father, thank You that You approve of celebrations and celebrating. Help us to be wise about the way we spend holidays, and may our family make many special memories to treasure. In Jesus' name, amen."

Devotion 126

Scripture:

"Each of you is to take up a stone on his shoulder . . . to serve as a sign among you. In the future, when your children ask you, 'What do these stones mean?' tell them . . . these are to be memorial to the people of Israel forever" (Joshua 4:5–7).

Some traditions are simply symbols of remembering, remembering what God has done for us. The verses above are about a symbol of remembering what God gave to Israel. One man from each tribe picked up a stone and placed it in a pile to make a memorial of the day they safely crossed the Jordan river. For us today, souvenirs, scrapbooks, and family photos help us to remember special events and recall celebrations of the past. To look at these reminders of a past event helps family members recall the times we have spent together. It gives our children a sense of shared history, a feeling of belonging together over time.

Do you keep scrapbooks or photo albums? If not for the family, perhaps you could give an inexpensive album to each child and divide up the pictures of vacations and parties among them. Take pictures of ordinary family activities, too, like raking leaves or playing in the snow, and put the pictures in the albums for making memories. Save a leaf in the album along with the pictures. We have some great photos of the kids and Dad digging out after a blizzard. When we see those pictures we remember that feeling of "us against the storm," the fun and boredom of snow days, and the coziness of our home.

Let's Talk:

Talk about things in your family that would be more fun and easier to remember if you had a souvenir or pictures of it. Would someone in the family want to be the designated photographer or scrapbook keeper?

To Learn More:

Read Joshua 4:1–9 for the whole story about the memorial of stones in the Jordan river.

Prayer:

"Dear Father God, thank You that You are at work in our family. Help us to think of special ways to remember what You do for us. In Jesus' name, amen."

Devotion 127

Scripture:

These days should be remembered and observed in every generation by every family . . . and these days of Purim should never cease to be celebrated by the Jews (Esther 9:28).

We said yesterday that traditions can help people remember what God has done for them. An example of this is the Jewish holiday of Purim. Queen Esther first made this a holiday in order to celebrate the deliverance of the Jews from the murderous plans of the wicked Haman. It was written that the Israelites should celebrate this time by "feasting and joy and giving presents . . . to one another and gifts to the poor" (Esther 9:22). This sounds something like the way Christmas is celebrated, doesn't it?

In our family, Halloween is a special holiday because that was the day the boys and I first met the girls, the day God brought our two families together. On that first Halloween of our courtship, the boys and I delivered a little party to the girls because they were sick with chicken pox and couldn't go out. We brought sloppy joes, carrot sticks, pretzels, and cider, along with a ceramic pumpkin for a center piece. To this day, eight Halloweens later, we use that same centerpiece and try to have those same foods on Halloween night. On Halloween, when we sit at the table with that centerpiece to eat those foods, we are remembering how it was the night we met. Doing the same thing each year has given our children a sense of continuity and shared history that they would not have if we didn't commemorate such events.

Let's Talk:

Do you remember special days in your family that are not necessarily special to others? Talk about your memories, especially your "firsts," and see if you can come up with a way to memorialize them. We are finding that as the years pass, not every one is there for every celebration. But our doing it and their knowing it happens increases the sense of family that we share.

To Learn More:

For the whole story about Purim, read Esther 9:18–32.

Prayer:

"Dear Father, thank You for bringing us together. Help us to find pleasant ways to remember what You have done for us. In Jesus' name, amen."

Devotion 128

Scripture:

The Lord said to Moses, "Say to the Israelites: On the first day of the seventh month you are to have a day of rest, a sacred assembly commemorated with trumpet blasts. Do no regular work, but present an offering made to the LORD" (Leviticus 23:23–25).

Talk about excuses to party! God told His children that on a certain day they should not do any work but have a party to get together and blast the trumpets! It seems pretty obvious that God wants His people to have party times, days to spend together for no reason except to rest from work and to give time to each other and to God.

We celebrate the specialness of each individual in our family with birthday parties. Some parties may be extensive, with lots of guests and decorations. We do one like that for the sixteenth birthday. For thirteenth birthdays we've usually had sleep-overs with a few friends, and for the fourteenth we take the family out to eat at a restaurant of the birthday person's choice. Most other birthdays are celebrated with just our family at home with a specially decorated table followed by cake and ice-cream. (I have a cupboard of supplies and decorations that I use over and over.) More often than not, the celebration doesn't even happen on the exact day of the birthday, but we celebrate it when we can. Why do we have such traditions for birthdays? For one thing, we like to party! But this is a wonderful way to celebrate the specialness of the individual and the togetherness of the family. There is something to be said for "at our house — we always." This is part of what defines us as a family.

Let's Talk:

How do you celebrate birthdays at your house? Maybe going out for Saturday brunch would be better for you. Maybe showering the person with homemade cards or gifts of favors such as "I will do your chores for a week" could take the place of buying gifts. It doesn't matter how or what you celebrate, the important thing is that you do. Talk about it, plan it, and do it.

To Learn More:

To get a feel for the other kinds of special days God gave to His people in the Old Testament, read the titles of the feast days in Leviticus chapters 23 through 25.

Prayer:

"Dear Jesus, help us to value one another as persons for whom You died. May we celebrate each other the way that You celebrate us. In Your name, amen."

Devotion 129

Scripture:
There will be trouble and distress for every human being who does evil . . . but glory, honor and peace for everyone who does good (Romans 2:9–10).

When we first got married, it was a time when the children felt a little confused about how valuable they were and what their places were in the new family. One of the ways to assure each child of his or her unique specialness was to have what we called "the kid of honor." After accomplishing something of importance such as being in a play, the end of ball season, getting the first A in a difficult subject, or getting that first "real" job, they would be honored. That means they would get to sit at the head of the table, pick the food and decorations for the table, and we would sing, "for he's (or she's) a jolly good fellow." Very simple things, but together as a family we were celebrating the worth of the individual and the specialness of their accomplishments. With time, and in light of all the birthdays we celebrate, this tradition has died out. But it was a great tool in the beginning of our family to assure the children that they had not lost their specialness (their honor) or their identity. Their accomplishments, which may have brought them more attention in a smaller family, were now a reason to celebrate in a bigger family.

Let's Talk:
If you aren't big on birthdays, are there other times and other ways that you can celebrate together? Listen to the children, see what is important to them. Make plans and do it! I challenge you to plan some memories into your family life and see your family bond and blend because of them.

To Learn More:
For further meditation, read Romans 14:5–8.

Prayer:
"Dear God, help us to remember that we do not live for ourselves alone, but we live together as a family for You. In Jesus' name, amen."

Devotion 130

Scripture:

If any of you lacks wisdom, he should ask God, who gives generously to all without finding fault, and it will be given to him (James 1:5).

"You can't be serious!" screamed Jennifer at her dad. "We always go to Grandma Jones's on the day before Christmas. Now you tell me we have to spend it with some strange people! Well, I don't want to go!"

Her dad felt awful. In trying to make time for both sets of parents during the holidays, he had forgotten about the grandparents this first Christmas of his new marriage. What could he do?

They called a family meeting. Jennifer's dad and stepmother made a list of all the traditional holiday get-togethers that Jennifer and her brother felt were important. They rated them in order of how strongly the children felt about them. Then they listed out the ones that were important to the stepmother's children. They looked them over and realized they would not be able to visit all the people they had visited before their marriage on the same special days. But with the help of all the parents and all the stepparents, they were able to come up with a holiday calendar. Part of adapting to their new family was learning that some things could stay the same and some things had to change.

Holidays and traditions are very important and usually very emotional issues. Try to understand the feelings of importance the parents or children have toward a given event and respond to those feelings. A tradition may not make sense. Why you always do it that way is not nearly as important as how strongly the child or parent feels about doing it. Pray for wisdom and guidance when making your holiday plans. Plan in advance so both the children and the adults have time to adapt mentally to the fact that "this year it will be different."

To blend and to bond you need to make your own memories and create some of your own unique family traditions. But never take away a tradition without supplying one in its place.

Let's Talk:

How has your family done in this area? What events are important to you during the holidays? Can you do everything that is important to all of you? Probably you can't. Decide which ones are the most important and do those. Visit the people you long to spend time with before and after the main holiday season.

To Learn More:

For further help in getting through this difficult adjustment, read James 1:2–8.

Prayer:

"Dear Lord, help us to be sensitive to one another's feelings. Most of all, help us to love one another. In Jesus' name, amen."

Devotion 131

Scripture:

One man considers one day more sacred than another . . . (Romans 14:5).

On our first Christmas together, we tried to do every single family celebration on all four sides of the family. Because some of the relatives didn't know how to respond to our blending, we got them off the hook by having the holiday gatherings at our house. We thought, "This will show them we still care about them and that our children are still a part of their family." While doing all that entertaining did fulfill it's purpose, I, as hostess and a mom who had suddenly more than doubled her number of children, became entirely exhausted. It wasn't worth it; some things had to "give." In the years since, we have learned to spread out the celebrating with special people all through the year.

For example, I have an aunt and uncle that mean a lot to me, a part of my family that I had traditionally seen at least once or twice a year, usually around Thanksgiving or Christmas. These people hold an important place in my heart, and I would not like to give up celebrating something with them. But knowing our blended family could not usually put a visit with them into the regular holiday schedule, I invented a new holiday to celebrate with my Aunt JoAnn and Uncle David. We have an "Apple Dinner." For this day, the table cloth is red, the centerpiece is a silver bowl of shiny apples, and we use all the best china. The food has an "appley" theme, such as waldorf salad, apple muffins, apple cake, apple-squash bake for a vegetable, and cider glaze for the ham. We have a nice celebration early in the fall, and I don't feel as if my new family circumstances have deprived me of spending time with this aunt and uncle that I love very much.

Let's Talk:

What do you like the best about Christmas? What do you like the best about Thanksgiving? Can you as a family keep doing the thing you like the best? Could you extend your holiday time? Sometimes having a late get-together in January or an early one in the fall will give you the time you need to enjoy all the important people in your life. Is it the get-together that's important? Or is the important thing seeing a certain aunt or a visit with a pair of cousins? Perhaps you could visit with them in a different way or at a different time. As with so many other issues, the important thing is "talk, talk, talk." Communicate about the importance certain events and people hold for each of you until you understand each other. Pray together for wisdom and God will give it!

To Learn More:

For further meditation, read Romans 14:7–8.

Prayer:

"Father God, please help us to understand what is important to each member of our family. Make us wise in how to do this blending. In Jesus' name, amen."

Devotion 132

Scripture:

Do not let any unwholesome talk come out of your mouths, but only what is helpful for building others up according to their needs, that it may benefit those who listen (Ephesians 4:29).

Sometimes it seems just impossible to communicate, especially stepparent to stepchildren. Lacking a shared history and without the special bonding that occurs in infancy, each may be amazed at the other's emotional response to an issue. But if both parents and children are determined to do what is good for the other, to act and speak in ways that build each other up, there will be a lot more peace and harmony in the family.

When having a disagreement, it helps to keep in mind that the relationship is more important than being right. Not that right doesn't need to be done, but being right in an argument isn't all there is to the issue. This verse tells us to think about what is good for the other person, what will build them up. Calling names and giving put-downs certainly doesn't build each other up. Every family will have disagreements; we have certainly had our share. Remembering not to call names, remembering not to do put-downs, and remembering to allow the other person their feelings on an issue are helpful "rules of fighting." But the most helpful fighting rule of all is remembering that the only "winner" is the relationship.

Let's Talk:

Can you remember an argument when the rules for good fighting made it better in the end? Can you remember a fight when it ended horribly? Was not remembering some of the things mentioned above one of the reasons it went so badly? Are you in the habit of fighting clean? If not, there may be too much pain between you to even discuss this subject. It may be one of those areas in which you need professional assistance to work it out.

To Learn More:

For further meditation, read Ephesians 4:29–5:1.

Prayer:

"Dear Father God, please empower us with Your Spirit to only do and say what is good for building each other up. In Jesus' name, amen."

Devotion 133

Scripture:

Each of us should please his neighbor for his good, to build him up (Romans 15:2).

I have often written notes to my children to build them up, notes of praise, recognition, or validation. If we have had angry words and even if we haven't resolved the issue in question, there is still a lot that is good and right about the person and about our relationship that can be reinforced. I have hung notes in lockers at school when the morning didn't get off to a good start and placed notes on dressers or beds for the child to see when he or she comes home. Doing this can change the whole mood of a relationship or tone of a person's day. A note works well for compliments and positive reinforcement because you can write it when you think of it. So often I have thought, "I need to tell so and so what a good job he or she did" and then I forget by the time I see the child. Taking time out to validate the good, to remind the other what you truly like about him or her can help the healing to start after a disagreement and make the other's sense of self-worth soar at any time.

Now my children have begun to write notes to me! Their notes of thanks or notes of affirmation make a whole lot of difference to my world. Positive words, fitly spoken, have been a great tool for growing and for improving relationships at our house.

Let's Talk:

Do you think you would like to get a note from your mom or dad? How do you think it would make you feel? Have you ever written a note to one of them? What happened? Be careful not to write anything down that could be hurtful.

To Learn More:

For further meditation, you may want to read the lovely proverb in Proverbs 25:11.

Prayer:

"Dear Lord, help us to genuinely try to do and say that which will build up each person in our family. Thank You for Your help in our relationships. In Jesus' name, amen."

Devotions for the Blended Family

Devotion 134

Scripture:

May the God of hope fill you with all joy and peace as you trust in him, so that you may overflow with hope by the power of the Holy Spirit (Romans 15:13).

Have you felt without hope? Have you ever been or are you now so burdened down with the way things are not blending well in your family that you just don't know how it can possibly work?

I have felt that way a few times. But I have changed my thinking, regained my hope, by filling my mind with promises from God's Word like the one in this verse. There is so much power in prayer and so much power in God's Word. After a time of praying very specifically for wisdom and after filling up on the promises of God's Word, I have seen hope and joy and peace restored in our family, even when none of the circumstances have changed. Sometimes hopelessness is nothing more than physical exhaustion, a virus, or poor exercise and sleeping patterns. Sometimes hopelessness is depression that needs professional counseling or medical treatment to be banished. But in all things and at all times, God will send His Spirit to comfort us if we trust in Him.

Let's Talk:

What makes you feel hopeless? Can the members of the family work together to keep this bad feeling away?

To Learn More:

For further meditation, read John 14:1, 27 and 2 Corinthians 4:8–9.

Prayer:

"Dear Holy Spirit, thank You for Your comforting presence that renews our hope. Thank You for being with us through another day and another night. In Jesus' name, amen."

Devotion 135

Scripture:

Let us therefore make every effort to do what leads to peace and to mutual edification (Romans 14:19).

This verse is a challenge for every family. If things have not been going the way you would like, whether you are a parent or a kid, maybe you need to "make every effort" to do things that lead to peace. "Mutual edification" means for the good of each other.

When we are having problems, we need to stop and think about what we really want. Are we just trying to get our own way?

Are we being selfish, or are we thinking about the good of the whole family? Sometimes what is good for one of us really isn't what is right for another or the rest of us. But someone who is "making every effort to do what leads to peace" will find a way to compromise or, if necessary, give up what he or she desires for the good of the family.

Let's Talk:

What are some things that would help the peace in your house? Can you each think or one or two things that you could do for the good of every other person in the family? Can you see how the mood of your home could change if each person did just one good thing for every other person? Try it!

To Learn More:

For further insight, read the "love chapter," 1 Corinthians 13.

Prayer:

"Dear Father in heaven, fill us with Your kind of love. May we purposefully set out to do things that are good for one another, and in this way may our family be strengthened. In Jesus' name and for Your glory we pray this, amen."

Devotion 136

Scripture:

For I am the Lord*, your God, who takes hold of your right hand and says to you, Do not fear; I will help you (Isaiah 41:13).*

One day when she was eleven years old, Lisa was asked to write a psalm for Bible class. The psalm she wrote expresses the truth of the verse above.

How empty I was, how lonely I was.
I was left with simple memories and pain.
I became alone, with only one leader, one guide.
How little I knew, how helpless I was,
    this life was unknown to me.
Then the Lord blessed me
    with more blessings than before.
Little pain I now feel
    for I have found more than I lost.
Praise the Lord!
For He has helped me in my confusion.
"I didn't call to You Lord, in my pain.
Yet You blessed me.
Though my sorrow was strong,
You increased my happiness."
I am thankful to God
He healed me of my scars.
Great is the Lord!
I am thankful to Him.

Let's Talk:

Have you ever felt God help you or comfort you even before you thought to call out to Him? Share with the family times when you may have felt the Lord taking you by the hand.

To Learn More:

For further meditation, read Isaiah 41:9–15.

Prayer:

"Dear Father, thank You for taking us by the hand and giving us comfort and strength. Thank You for Your comforting love. In Your most precious and holy name, amen."

Devotion 137

Scripture:

"Then you will call upon me and come and pray to me, and I will listen to you. You will seek me and find me when you seek me with all your heart. I will be found by you," declares the Lord (Jeremiah 29:12–14).

Yesterday, I asked if you could think of a time when you felt the comforting presence of the Lord, a time when He took you by the hand. Maybe there never has been a time when you felt the Lord like that. Today's verse assures us that if you seek the Lord "with all your heart," you will find Him.

Let's Talk:

What do you think it means to seek after God "with all your heart"? Have you sought the Lord this way? Share those times with your family. If you have not had a seeking and a finding of the Lord in your life, pray for each other that you will. There is nothing like His comforting presence, but He is only real to those who have sought and found Him.

To Learn More:

For further meditation, read Jeremiah 29:10–14.

Prayer:

"Dearest Lord Jesus, thank You that You promise to be found by those who seek You with all of their hearts. Thank You that You never leave or forsake Your children, even when we don't feel Your presence. In Your name, amen."

Devotion 138

Scripture:
Does he [God] not see my ways and count my every step? (Job 31:4).

Kim sat on her bed and dashed hurt and angry tears from her eyes. She was going down to the living room to watch TV when she saw her dad dancing around the room with her stepmother. She couldn't stand it! That woman was such a klutz! Her mother had been such a graceful dancer, and her mom and dad had always enjoyed dancing together. When they danced, they were graceful and looked beautiful. Now her father was laughing and stumbling around the room with someone else in his arms. Kim didn't think she could ever get used to her dad being with another woman.

"Why, oh, why did Mom have to die? Why did Dad have to get married again?" she thought. She cried until she fell asleep.

What Kim didn't know was that in time, her pain would ease up. In time, while never forgetting her mother, she would come to care for and depend upon her stepmother. No, it would never be "the same." But it could be wonderful. This new life had to be lived just like the old one—one step at a time.

Let's Talk:
What are some steps you have taken to care for and depend upon your stepmom or stepdad?

To Learn More:
For further meditation, read Psalm 103:11–18.

Prayer:
"Dear Lord Jesus, thank You that all our steps are seen by You. Help us to trust You, even when we don't understand. Thank You for the comforting presence of the Holy Spirit. Amen."

Devotion 139

Scripture:

If it is possible, as far as it depends on you, live at peace with everyone (Romans 12:18).

Mom and some of the kids were trying to talk to each other after school one day. But the pounding and blare of music was so loud they had to raise their voices to talk.

Mom called to Aaron, "Please turn the music down!" No response. She went to the intercom and turning it high, yelled, "Turn the music down!" It got quiet. Now, all they could hear was the pounding of the bass.

The family can never predict what sounds will come from Aaron's room. He likes classical music, pop, and rock, as well as alternative rock and oldies. As long as it has good lyrics and real musical quality, he listens to it. But all of it, even classical and religious, has to be LOUD! He says that he wants to "feel" it as well as hear it.

While this may be a fine hobby for Aaron, it can create problems for the family. The house is not large, and a large family living together requires a high degree of thoughtfulness. In this situation, very loud noise in the background certainly does not contribute to a peaceful atmosphere. Sometimes, in his love for the music, Aaron forgets that what he listens to can either contribute to or detract from the peace of the household.

Let's Talk:

Do you have a passion the creates conflict between you and the ones with whom you live? What things do each of you do that infringe on the space of others? Can you think of a way to enjoy your hobby without violating the peace of others? Talking about it before the conflict occurs is very helpful.

To Learn More:

For further insight on how to get along, you may like to read Colossians 3:12–15.

Prayer:

"Dear Father in heaven, please help us to love each other more, and to be considerate one to another. In Jesus' name we pray. Amen."

Devotion 140

Scripture:
"Do to others as you would have them do to you" (Luke 6:31).

"Get those earrings out of your ears right now!" yelled Becky at her sister Lisa. "M-o-m! Would you tell Lisa to leave my stuff alone? Yesterday she wore my sweater and today she's wearing my earrings! She never asks me!"

Mom and Dad sat down with Lisa and Becky and had a talk. The girls share a room, and sometimes they have mutually owned certain items of clothing. Both of these conditions made Lisa feel that she could get into Becky's things and use them. Becky didn't think she should have to share everything she owned with her sister. Lisa pointed out that Becky often borrowed her clothing, too. "But," Becky says, "I usually ask you first."

"You didn't yesterday," retorted Lisa.

"But you weren't here to ask," snapped her sister.

Mom and Dad decided to set limits. There would be certain special possessions that could never be borrowed by someone else. Everything else could not be borrowed without permission. If the owner wasn't there, the item could not be used. Of course the limits have been transgressed at times, so there has to be a consequence. For example, when Lisa took Becky's earrings without asking, she was grounded from wearing any earrings, including her own, for a week. The consequence helped her to remember. These guidelines have created a lot more peace between the girls.

Let's Talk:
Have you ever had a problem with property rights at your house? Have you tried setting limits? Have you thought of the consequences of violating those limits? If you have never done this, do you think it would help if you did?

To Learn More:
For further insight on getting along, read Luke 6:31–36.

Prayer:
"Dear Father, help us to love one another and treat each other the way we want to be treated. In Jesus' name, amen."

Devotions for the Blended Family

Devotion 141

Scripture:
Carry each other's burdens, and in this way you will fulfill the law of Christ (Galatians 6:2).

When we married, the girls' grandfather on their mother's side was already very old. Within a couple of years of our marriage, he died. Even though the boys and I had not known him a long time like Roger and the girls had, we grieved with them and offered them our comfort and support. Almost exactly one year later, the boys' grandfather on their father's side also died. Now it was Roger and the girls' turn to be there as the boys and I grieved for this father-in-law and grandpa that we deeply loved. It doesn't matter if we all share the same feelings of loss. It doesn't matter that one spouse and some of the children have a history with the deceased and the other spouse and rest of the children don't. What counts is that when one member of the family hurts, the others are there to comfort that one and help carry the burden of his or her grief. That may mean standing around a funeral home with lots of people you don't know and listening to teary folks share family stories of which you were not a part. But that's okay. You can do it for the sake of people you love and are committed to—your blended family.

Let's Talk:
Have you shared a grief experience in your family? Have you felt shut out because you didn't share the same feelings of grief? Remember that you can share in a person's pain, even if you don't have exactly the same feelings yourself.

To Learn More:
For further meditation, read 2 Corinthians 1:3–7.

Prayer:
"Dear Lord Jesus, thank You for Your love and the comforting presence of the Holy Spirit when we hurt. May we always love and comfort one another as You have loved and comforted us. In Your name, amen."

Devotion 142

Scripture:

"For God so loved the world that he gave his one and only Son, that whoever believes in him shall not perish but have eternal life" (John 3:16).

Lisa and Becky were very sad, maybe even a little tearful. Oscar the chameleon was dead. He had lived a long and contented lizard life; even the pet store keeper said they had taken good care of him. The girls had enjoyed letting him run up and down their arms, watch him play, and do silly lizardy things. But chameleons don't have a very long life-expectancy. And when they die, they are dead. They return to the ground, turn to dust, and that's the end of it.

When people die, they also return to the earth. But there is a big difference between a lizard and a person, and the difference is greater than intelligence and life awareness. The difference is that people have souls. Every person has one. You can't see or touch a soul. It is the "real you," the part inside that feels, loves, and worships God. When a person dies, the body returns to the earth, but the soul goes on living. Dying is a part of life; everyone must die sometime. But dying is not the end of living.

This verse tells us that when we accept Jesus Christ as our Savior, we belong to God's family. When we die, our souls will go to heaven. Someday God will give us new bodies, and we will live with Him—forever. Heaven is the presence of God, a happy place where no one is ever sick or sad. It is the hope of heaven and the knowledge that our loved ones loved God and believed in Jesus that comforts us when we think about how much we miss them.

Let's Talk:

Have you ever had a pet that died? How did it make you feel? Does concentrating on the good memories instead of always thinking about the loss make you feel better? If you have loved ones that have died, does it help to remember the good times?

To Learn More:

To learn more about heaven, read Revelation 21:1–5 and Revelation 7:13–17. If you are curious about the soul part of you, you may want to read these verses: Genesis 1:27 and 2:7 and Matthew 10:29.

Prayer:

"Dear Jesus, thank You for dying on the cross to take the punishment for all that I have done wrong. Thank You that because of this, I can live forever in heaven with You. Amen."

Devotion 143

Scripture:

Love is patient, love is kind. It does not envy, it does not boast, it is not proud (1 Corinthians 13:4).

Sometimes when stepsiblings go to see the grandparents that they do not share in common, they may come home with presents that are not for sharing. Sometimes an aunt or an uncle may take you out to lunch or dinner or give you a treat, and your stepbrother or stepsister doesn't get to go or get to have the treat. Sometimes you may go to visit your other birth parent. He or she may give you things and take you places, and of course the stepsiblings at home do not get to do the same. This is one of the very toughest things about being kids in a blended family.

Some thoughts that may help you are found in this verse. When it is other people who are getting the treat, try to be happy for them and share in the joy of their seeing their other parent or relative. Just as we talked about sharing in sorrow in Devotion 141, we can also share in joy. If you are the person who got the treat, don't flaunt it or brag or tease about it.

Let's Talk:

Has this sort of thing ever happened in your family? Have you ever felt jealous of what the other kids got? Can you tell them how it made you feel? Can you think of ways to help each other feel better? If you don't get taken out by relatives and your stepbrother or stepsister does, perhaps your parents could adopt a grandparent or aunt or uncle for you. Perhaps one set of kids' visitation time could be "parents treat time" with the kids who don't get to go. Remember, think of the other person and his or her feelings. Think about it now, ahead of time, so you will be ready to act with love when the time comes.

To Learn More:

For further meditation, read Romans 12:9–10.

Prayer:

"Dear Lord Jesus, help us to love one another as You have loved us. In Your name, amen."

Devotion 144

Scripture:
A friend loves at all times (Proverbs 17:17).

Every day, Chelsie came to play with Sally. She loved jumping on Sally's trampoline. Each day the girls spent time together, jumping and giggling and talking. But fall came and it was time to take down the trampoline tarp for the winter. When Sally answered Chelsie's knock at the door the day after the tramp was put away, she said, "Come on in, let's go to my room and play with my dolls."

"Why can't we jump on your trampoline like we always do?" whined Chelsie.

"It's put away for the winter. But we could play games or draw if you don't want to play dolls," offered Sally.

"I hate dolls and games and everything! I don't want to be your friend anymore!" And Chelsie huffed away.

Chelsie is what is called a "fair weather friend." As long as everything is going fine, as long as she gets her way and there are no problems, she is a friend. But as soon as something changes, or there is a problem, she's gone. She shows that she is not really a friend at all.

Let's Talk:
Have you ever had a friend like Chelsie? Have you ever acted like Chelsie? How can you be a good friend to others?

To Learn More:
For further meditation, read Psalm 41:9–13.

Prayer:
"Dear Lord, please help us to be good and faithful friends. Help us to love one another the way that You love us. In Jesus' name, amen."

Devotion 145

Scripture:

A man of many companions may come to ruin, but there is a friend who sticks closer than a brother (Proverbs 18:24).

Do your friends sometimes get you into trouble? This proverb tells us that many friendships can be bad, many companions may lead us to ruin. But a true friend, a good friend, is faithful, so faithful that he sticks closer than a brother. That means that not only is he or she always there when needed, but also that such a friend is there for your good. Many commentators of the Bible feel that the "friend who sticks closer than a brother" is Jesus. He certainly never leaves us, and everything He does is for our good. What could be more faithful than that?

In the Old Testament times, the influence of friends was taken very seriously. According to Jewish law, if a friend led you to worship other gods, you were to kill him! (You can read about this in Dueteronomy 13:6–9). I am not suggesting the same! But the point is, it is very important who our friends are. Do they strengthen our relationship with God? Or, do they lead us to "ruin" and away from God?

Let's Talk:

Has hanging around with the wrong friends ever gotten you to do something you would not have done otherwise? Sometimes you may think that they are the only friends available to you. But if you get involved in groups, clubs, or activities that you enjoy (and you may have to try a few before you know what you really like), you will make new friends.

To Learn More:

For examples of two wonderful friendships in the Bible, read 2 Samuel 18:1–4 and Philippians 2:19–20.

Prayer:

"Dear Jesus, thank You that You are always a faithful and true friend. Please provide for us the friends we need, friends that will be faithful, and good for us. Help us to be good friends to others. In Your name and for Your glory we pray. Amen."

Devotion 146

Scripture:

. . . if I have a faith that can move mountains, but have not love, I am nothing. If I give all I possess to the poor and surrender my body to the flames, but have not love, I gain nothing (1 Corinthians 13:2-3).

1 Corinthians 13 is called the "love chapter" of the Bible. In this beautiful prose we are impressed with how important it is to love. The verses that I picked out for today remind us just how important it is to love one another. We can have all kinds of power and wealth, we can do all kinds of good and wonderful things, but if we don't love God and we don't love one another, nothing we do amounts to anything at all.

It's not always easy to love. Because we are human and not perfect, we get hurt and offended. In our selfishness we hurt and offend others. Many times in this book we have talked about forgiveness. Forgiveness and love are alike in a way— that is, sometimes we just have to make up our minds and do it. Love sometimes must simply be a decision we make.

Let's Talk:

Have you ever been so hurt that you felt you could not ever love the person who hurt you again? Have you ever asked God and felt Him fill you with love? Sometimes, for our safety and well-being, we have to end relationships with people who have hurt us. Do you think it is possible to sever ties with someone and still forgive that person?

To Learn More:

For further meditation, read John 15:9–16.

Prayer:

"Dear Jesus, fill us with Your Spirit that we may love one another. In Your name we ask this. Amen."

Devotion 147

Scripture:

Love is patient, love is kind. It does not envy, it does not boast, it is not proud. It is not rude, it is not self-seeking, it is not easily angered, it keeps no record of wrongs. Love does not delight in evil but rejoices with the truth. It always protects, always trust, always hopes, always perseveres. Love never fails (1 Corinthians 13:4–8).

The above portion from the love chapter describes beautiful, perfect love. What are some of the things perfect love *does not* do?

Have you ever done those things? Of course you have; we all have!

What are some of the things perfect love *does* do? When have you, in your blended family, been patient and kind? When have you protected, trusted, hoped, and persevered?

Let's Talk:

Talk about the times when your love for one another has been really great, like some of these ideals. Can you forgive each other when your love has been less than ideal?

To Learn More:

For further thoughts on love, you may want to read the whole love chapter through.

Prayer:

"Dear Jesus, live in us, that we may love one another more perfectly. In Your name, and for Your glory, amen."

Devotion 148

Scripture:
Love never fails (1 Corinthians 13:8).

Yesterday we talked about some of the characteristics of perfect love. I wanted to mention it one more time as a reminder that no one loves perfectly except God. Our human love does fail, but with God in us we can love one another more perfectly.

While I said two days ago that sometimes you must make the decision to love, it is also true that you cannot really love, in the way described in the Bible, unless you have the Holy Spirit of God living within you. According to 1 John 4:7 it is from God that true and pure love comes.

The following are some of the love facts found throughout the New Testament. John 13:35 says that the followers of Jesus are to be known by their love for one another. John 14:15 says that if we love God, we will keep His commandments. And 1 John 4:21 says that if you love God, you will love each other.

Let's Talk:
Answer these questions silently, in your own heart. Do I love God? If I think that I love God, do I love my brothers and sisters? If I think that I love God, do I keep His commandments? What does that tell me about my love for God? Does your love for God need to grow?

To Learn More:
For a reminder of how we will act if we love God, read 1 John 2:4–6.

Prayer:
"Dear Jesus, help us each day to give up more of ourselves to You. As our love for You grows, may we grow in our love for one another. Help us to continue in Your love all of our days. In Your name, and by Your power we pray. Amen."

Devotion 149

Scripture:

I appeal to you, brothers, in the name of our Lord Jesus Christ, that all of you agree with one another so that there may be no divisions among you and that you may be perfectly united in mind and thought (1 Corinthians 1:10).

What a verse for a blended family! The apostle Paul wrote this to Christians in a church who were letting their differences get between them. He appealed to them that through the power of Jesus Christ, they should put their differences aside and agree to be united. We may not agree on certain things. But if we do agree that our focus needs to be more on our unity than on our differences, we can make our relationships work. Remember the rules for good fighting (Devotion 132)? The relationship is more important than being right. Everyone, especially the mom and the dad, must be committed to this in order for it to work.

Let's Talk:

Are you dealing with major differences between you right now? Can you compromise? If you can't, you may want to get a person to be a go-between for you the way the apostle Paul was for the Corinthian church. But it may come down to this final thing—that you simply must put aside your differences and make up your minds to get along.

To Learn More:

For further meditation, you may want to once again read the love chapter, 1 Corinthians 13.

Prayer:

"Dear Father, please fill our home with Your peace. Help us to be united in heart and keep our unity as a family preserved, so that within it we may all feel loved and secure. In Jesus' name, amen."

Devotion 150

Scripture:
Accept one another, then, just as Christ accepted you, in order to bring praise to God (Romans 15:7).

At the beginning of this book we talked about how a blended family is what it is: parts of other families coming together to make a new family unit, parts making a new whole, truly a family but truly always blended. It's okay that we are what we are and not something else. The challenge is to make this group, these parts, harmonize and blend. In order to do that, we must be accepting and loving. God loved us while we were still in our sins (Romans 5:8), and we must love one another the way that He loved us. Christ died for us and bears with us in our weaknesses and struggles and remains compassionate toward us. How much more do we, in a blended family, need to be compassionate and patient and kind with one another. We do this for the security and peace of the individuals in our family, to get along together, and to make our family work. But most of all we behave in this way in order to bring praise and glory to God.

In all the things that we have talked about in this book and in all the struggles we have attempted to resolve, one thing remains obvious—none of this works without love and compassionate acceptance of each member of this family by every other member.

Let's Talk:
Have there been times when you felt unaccepted by this family or someone in this family? Have there been times when you were not patient and kind to someone else? Rather than arguing now about who was right or wrong, what would happen if you decided to be loving and kind in the same way that Jesus was?

To Learn More:
For further meditation, read Romans 15:1–13.

Prayer:
"Dear Father God, please pour out Your Spirit, that we may accept and love one another the way that You have loved and accepted us. In Jesus' name, and for Your glory we pray. Amen."

Devotion 151

Scripture:

May the God who gives endurance and encouragement give you a spirit of unity among yourselves as you follow Christ Jesus, so that with one heart and mouth you may glorify the God and Father of our Lord Jesus Christ (Romans 15:5–6).

What do you think it means that God gives "endurance and encouragement"? Have you asked Him for them? Have you seen Christ Jesus give you a spirit of unity as you follow Him in your daily lives? If your family lacks a spirit of unity, do you think following Jesus (that is, doing as He would do to each other) would help make unity grow? When you do have unity, when your family is going well, do you glorify God?

Let's Talk:

Take a moment right now to thank God for bringing you together and for helping you blend.

To Learn More:

For further thoughts on unity, read Psalm 133:1–3.

Prayer:

"Dear Father God, thank You for Your grace to us. We, in our blended family, with one heart and one voice, do glorify You and bless Your name for all that You are and all that You have done for us. Thank You. In Jesus' name, amen."

Devotion 152

. . . .

Scripture:

I will sing and make music with all my soul. . . .I will praise you, O LORD, among the nations; I will sing of you among the peoples. For great is your love, higher than the heavens; your faithfulness reaches to the skies. Be exalted, O God, above the heavens, and let your glory be over all the earth (Psalm 108:1–5).

Some days, as we sit at the table and enjoy one another's company, as we tease and roughhouse and share our days, we are still so happy to be together. No, having a second marriage did not fix everything that was wrong in life. But it has given a father to my boys and a mother to Rog's girls. We are not a perfect family. We still struggle, as does any family, with how to take all our differences and stick them together to make a whole unit. But we are so glad that in His faithfulness, God brought us together and made us what we are: a blended family.

Let's Talk:

What are some of the happiest memories of your blended family? What do you thank God for the very most?

To Learn More:

For further meditation on God's faithfulness, read Psalm 105:1–5.

Prayer:

"Dear God, how we praise You, how we exalt You; may our family always bring glory to Your name. Amen."

. . . .

Index of Topics